The Complete Book of
GARDEN SEATING

The Complete Book of
GARDEN SEATING

45
Great
Projects
from
Wood
Stone
Metal
Fabric
& more

Janice Eaton Kilby

LARK BOOKS

A Division of Sterling Publishing Co., Inc.

Art Direction and Production: **Dana Margaret Irwin**
Computer Illustrations and Production Assistance: **Hannes Charen and Orrin Lundgren**
Assistant Editors: **Veronika Alice Gunter and Heather Smith**
Editorial Assistants: **Roper Cleland and Emma Jones**
Photography: **Evan Bracken**
Illustrations: **Olivier Rollin**

Library of Congress Cataloging-in-Publication Data
Kilby, Janice Eaton
   The complete book of garden seating : 40 great projects from wood,
stone, metal, fabric, found objects, and more / Janice Eaton Kilby.— 1st
ed.

     p. cm.
  ISBN 1-57990-209-X (hard)
   1. Garden ornaments and furniture—Design and construction. I. Title.

SB473.5 .K55 2001
684.1'8—dc21   00-064081

10 9 8 7 6 5 4 3 2 1
First Edition

Published by Lark Books, a division of
Sterling Publishing Co., Inc.
387 Park Avenue South
New York, N.Y. 10016

© 2001, Lark Books

Distributed in Canada by Sterling Publishing,
c/o Canadian Manda Group, One Atlantic Ave., Suite 105
Toronto, Ontario, Canada M6K 3E7

Distributed in Australia by Capricorn Link (Australia) Pty Ltd.,
P.O. Box 6651, Baulkham Hills, Business Centre NSW 2153, Australia

Distributed in the U.K. by Guild of Master Craftsman Publications Ltd.,
Castle Place 166 High Street, Lewes, East Sussex, England, BN7 1XU.
Tel: (+44) 1273 477374 • Fax: (+44) 1273 478606
Email: pubs@thegmcgroup.com • Web: www.gmcpublications.com

If you have questions or comments about this book, please contact:
Lark Books
50 College Street
Asheville, North Carolina 28801
(828) 253-0467

Manufactured in Hong Kong by Dai Nippon Printing, Ltd..

ISBN 1-57990-209-X

Table of Contents

Introduction

The places we love most outdoors, and what we do when we're out there, say a great deal about us. Sometimes we're drawn to grand views, secret resting places in the woods, or places that enlarge our sense of the world. Other times, safe in the privacy of our backyard, we putter around the garden, eager to see what tiny, new surprises have arrived since yesterday.

Have you noticed how many gardeners create imaginative plantings and inviting layouts, but their nerve fails when it comes to seating? Many people design and plant wonderful gardens, but they think it's much too hard or complicated to make their own

outdoor seating. Wrong! Whether you have two acres of landscaped gardens or—like most of us—a compact backyard with a flowerbed, you can make seating that's perfect for your own special place outdoors and have fun doing it!

There are some classic seating designs that work so well they'll be used and loved forever, and they're in this book. Who doesn't love roomy Adirondack chairs with armrests that are actually designed to hold arms (and a drink, and a book) comfortably? How many of us still cherish warm childhood memories of the fan-backed metal lawn chairs and squeaky gliders that resided in our grandmothers' gardens? Maybe it's time to look at our own gardens again with childlike eyes, in the same spirit of play!

Give yourself permission to approach ideas about garden seating with freedom. Many a weary gardener has turned over a milk crate or tipped a wheelbarrow upright to make an instant seat from which to contemplate the day's work. A visitor to a

favorite view in the woods might bring only a cushion to put on a flat stone that's already perfect for sitting. Simple ideas are frequently the best, and easy is good.

The Complete Book of Garden Seating contains seating projects for readers at all skill levels. You'll learn how to create seating classics that last, including comfortable chairs,

In addition, we'll give you useful suggestions about how to choose seating that works for you, how to decide where to put it, and how to build and plant easy structures to give your seating areas shade and privacy. We've also added page after page of luscious garden photographs to delight and inspire you.

Your garden is waiting for you...

So, go on. Take this book with you and go outside. Your garden is waiting for you, and now you have some fabulous outdoor seating to make.

benches, loveseats, lounges, swings, and tree surrounds. The how-to projects feature a wide range of materials, handsome and witty designs, and surface treatments ranging from the traditional to the unexpected.

Don't fret if you already have a plain concrete bench, or—admit it—white plastic deck chairs. This book will help you re-envision and redecorate what you already have with projects like the Plastic Deck Chair Covers on page 142. Do you want fun ideas for using ready-made seating? Check out Circle Your Wagons on page 28. Would you like to try your hand at building a simple wooden bench along the edge of your flowerbed? See the Garden Perimeter Bench on page 103. Do you want a garden with a sense of humor? You can accessorize it with Giant Hibiscus Pillows on page 162.

Chapter I

Function, Form, and Easy Style

Establishing a personal style in your garden means following your own "rules" of creativity, freedom, and ease. When you create a garden for yourself, with seating that appeals to your own needs and feelings, you'll create a place that delights everyone. The word paradise, after all, comes from the ancient Persian word *pairi-daeza*. *Pairi* means around, and *daeza* means wall; together they translate into a walled garden, or the garden as heaven on earth.

Where does garden seating fit into your own bit of heaven on earth? A garden seat can be, and do, several things. It establishes a point of view from which you can enjoy a natural scene or a picture you've composed with the elements of your garden. If visitors to your garden sit down to rest and take a look at what's in front of them, it's a way of saying, "Look at

Jimmy Straehla, *Lucky,* 1999, 55 x 48 x 28 in. (139.7 x 122 x 71 cm); antique heart pine, lath, granite, copper wire, bottlecaps, old ceiling tin; sawn, nailed, wired.
PHOTO BY RINNE ALLEN

what I see. Isn't it wonderful?" In addition, outdoor seating gives us a place to enjoy the companionship of friends and family, or to cherish a moment of quiet solitude. Your garden seating is also an object to be enjoyed for its own visual appeal and comfort, and hand-crafting it yourself will give you a feeling of satisfaction very, very different from buying a mass-produced object that's literally one of a million.

Far left: Teri Stewart and Serey Andree, *Snake in Fig Tree,* 2000, 12 in. x 10 ft. (30.5 cm x 3 m); fabric, sequins; sewn, glued, painted.
PHOTO BY JANICE EATON KILBY

Form Follows Function

Before you select seating for your garden or alter what's there, the most important question to ask yourself is, "What do I like to do outside?" Do you dream of a hidden, quiet area where you can go for extended contemplation (sometimes also known as hiding or sleeping)? Then plant some shrubbery and prune it to form a shady hideaway for an armchair or chaise lounge (only one, please, or you'll defeat your purpose). Is there a natural stopping point on a path you walk frequently, or a little nook where you can tuck a bench for a delightful surprise as a stroller rounds a corner? Do you enjoy open-air conversations or eating outdoors? Then carry meals outside for dinner al fresco in chairs with arms wide enough to hold a plate of food and a drink. Do you and your guests always seem to end up outside when you have a party? You can accumulate pillows or lightweight, compact seating that's easy to set up and to store. Do you like to take a book or lap-

top computer outside to work? Then find a shady spot to reduce glare. Maybe you just want to escape from "doing" anything constructive. If you have a sturdy tree limb available, a swing is the perfect answer for grown-up play!

Location, Location, Location

The size and location of your garden seating will have to work with the available space, views, exposure (the direction you're facing, as shown on a compass), sun and shade at different times of day, and natural traffic patterns. Think about the seasons you use the garden, the times of day you're most likely to be in it, what you do in it when you get there, and where the most frequently travelled and most isolated spots are.

When do you use your garden the most? Do you like to move garden furnishings around to enjoy different aspects and views as the seasons change? If so, choose seats in portable materials and designs. Are you always shifting your chair to chase

Center right: After a home renovation, these gardeners used pieces from an old bathroom tile floor to enliven their garden.

available shade at different times of day? You might consider building an easy shade structure in a hot spot, or a portable canopy. Do you usually go out to your garden in the evening, after work? You may want to position a bench to face west, to enjoy the sunset. Asking these questions will help you decide what kind of seating best meets your needs. And remember, comfort counts above all. Lovely as it might be, you won't want to put a backless stone bench in a spot where you'd rather curl up on a chaise lounge with the Sunday paper.

You can also use structures such as arbors, hedges, and planted screens to create privacy and shelter for your seating and to divide up space and define a series of outdoor "rooms." When we're outdoors, we instinctively like to sit with our backs to a wall or a sheltering structure, and to be situated on top of a slight incline that looks out over the surrounding area. A garden seat is a handy device to direct attention to a view and to act as a focal point itself, an object that draws the eye to its placement in the garden. It gets your attention and beckons you closer.

The Ground Beneath Your Feet

The first time you have to extract the legs of a garden bench from muddy ground (where they sank when you sat down after a hard rain) you'll understand the benefit of choosing or preparing a site for your garden seat. You want the seat to rest on packed dirt, a layer of loose, nonporous material such as gravel, or a hard surface. It's also better for wood furniture not to be in direct contact with the ground, unless the wood has been chemically-treated for that purpose. You might want to highlight your seating by creating a discrete area of gravel, pebbles, bark, or wood chips around and under the seat.

If you're lucky, nature has done the floor decorations for you with native ground-cover, or you can plant a living "floor" underfoot that highlights the seating design. Inquire at a local nursery or

Left: Eric O'Leary, Tariki Studio, 1990, *stoneware ceramic garden seats,* **18 x 16 x 14 inches (45.7 x 40.6 x 35.6 cm).**
Courtesy of John Cram, Asheville, NC
PHOTO BY EVAN BRACKEN

Left: Sometimes it's fun to place the legs of a garden seat so your feet actually rest in low-altitude plants and flowers when you're taking your leisure.

Try intermingling flowers and scented herbs with patches of gravel or brick pavers laid into the ground.

Above: These "Diamond Chairs" are considered modern classics. Made of wire coated with vinyl, they were designed for Knoll International by Harry Bertoia in 1952.

garden center to determine the varieties best for your location. If your garden contains a moist, shady area with compacted, poorly drained, high-acid soil, you have a perfect environment to create a wonderful moss "carpet" for your seating. You can also create a moss floor by transplanting palm-size pieces of moss. Prepare the ground by clearing away all existing growth and watering it until it's muddy. Water the moss patch, press it to the ground, water again, then walk on it.

Material Possibilities

Most commercially available garden furniture is made of wood, iron, steel, aluminum, plastic, or concrete, and its designs are often inspired by world-famous "classics" (see page 21). Your choices in garden seating expand dramatically, however, when you decide to make your own, and it's a wonderful way to infuse your garden with your own personal style!

First, take a look at what you've got. Do you have a plain concrete bench? Apply a marvelous mosaic design as shown on the Botanical Mosaic Garden Bench on page 78. Is there a tree trunk in the garden, just waiting to be topped with the backrest from an old, legless chair? See the directions for our Beauty and the Beast Chair on page 33, and voila, you're on easy seat!

With the right tools, any material that makes a good surface to sit on, or that can support a surface to sit on, is fair game to become one-of-a-kind garden seating! Choice of materials is determined by your own taste, your analysis of what you want in your garden, portability, the level of maintenance required, durability, and comfort. In each chapter, we'll discuss the unique characteristics and relative merits of lumber, rustic wood, cement, living plants, bamboo, metal, found objects, brick, stone, and fabric.

Color, Scale, and other Rules to be Broken

Knowing how the human eye works can be helpful in seating decisions. You can use scale and color to affect the visual perception of an outdoor space. If you have a long, narrow garden with a bowling-alley feel, you can install a bright-colored or oversize seat at the most distant point, to draw the eye and visually "shorten" the garden. You can also use scale to play with perspective. By planting tiny, delicate foliage and flowers close to the seat from which you survey your garden, and locating big, coarse-leafed plants at the far end, you'll visually "shrink" the expanse. But don't be afraid to play with scale just for fun, either. Whimsical elements can make your garden a place of charm and true delight.

A rich color can make a commonplace piece of garden furniture look special, and it's a wonderful way to transform flea market finds into gorgeous garden accents. Purists recommend blues, grays, and blacks to help garden furniture recede into their surroundings, plus the occasional daring red as a focal point. But who said anything about being a purist? Use the colors you like to echo or contrast with nearby flowers or other blocks of color, and don't

WORRYING ABOUT WHETHER YOU CAN PUT MAGENTA NEXT TO RED IS FOR SISSIES.

Katherine Bernstein and Richard Kennedy, cast granite aggregate sculpture, 10 x 11 x 13 1/2 inches (25.4 x 27.9 x 34.3 cm). *Courtesy of Norma Cheren, Atlanta, GA.* PHOTO BY JANICE EATON KILBY

be afraid to be bold. Worrying about whether you can put magenta next to red is for sissies. When you furnish and decorate your garden, making an unusual or surprising choice is exactly how you define your own style.

In general, bright, hot colors such as orange and red stimulate and excite us, while pastels, blues, and greens feel soothing and calming. White intensifies the color of adjacent objects and flowers, and gray and silver help moderate the transition from one color to the next. But just remember, the most important rule about using color is to choose what pleases you!

CLASSICS OF GARDEN SEATING

by Enid Munroe

Classics stand the test of time, and garden seating is no exception. Did you know that the bench or chair you already have in your garden may be based on famous designs that are hundreds of years old?

Until the 16th century, people used to enjoy gardens as places to walk, but not to sit. The familiar bench supported by carved trestle legs (photo 1 on page 22) first appeared during the Italian Renaissance. Marble versions were used in the gardens of the villas of the Medicis, the fabulously rich, aristocratic Florentine family. The benches were carefully sited, placed against bound-

ary walls or at the end of a vista. We most often see this bench today made of cast concrete.

Stone turf benches covered with the herb chamomile first appeared in Elizabethan England, the time of England's own renaissance. Constructed of stone and earth, the benches are highly decorative and fragrant, though not very inviting to sit on. Photo 2 on page 22 shows the chamomile bench at Sissinghurst, the famous Kentish country estate. Made from old bits of masonry, the bench graces the herb garden.

— 2 —

— 3 —

— 4 —

— 5 —

Do you have a cast iron garden bench? Wrought iron garden furniture first appeared in the 18th century. Featuring ornate botanical details such as ferns, lilies, and grapevines, they had great ornamental and nostalgic appeal. By the 19th century, newly prosperous entrepreneurs of the Industrial Revolution were buying mass-produced cast-iron versions (see photo 3 and the photo on page 21).

— 1 —

Mass production created other types of metal garden seating. Chairs (photos 4 and 5) were made of wire or metal bent into intricately scrolled designs that gently molded to the body of the sitter. Nineteenth-century European park chairs (photo 6), with their small seats and straight backs, are treasured when they can be found.

In the 18th and 19th centuries, iron garden furniture makers frequently copied the work of the famous 18th-century English furniture designer, Thomas Chippendale. He incorporated Gothic, French rococo, and Chinese motifs in his work, and reproduction Chinese Chippendale benches of today (photo 7) still feature elaborate geometric designs.

Rustic furniture crafted from tree limbs, roots, branches, and twigs emerged as a reaction against formal, French-influenced design, at the same time that the famous landscape designer Capability Brown was creating vast natural parks in the English countryside. Rustic design exploits wood's graining, bark, burls, forks, and other oddities. By the mid-1800s, the "new rich" of the Industrial Revolution were also building country retreats furnished in rustic style. Victorians also encouraged ivy and vines to grow around tree stump "stools."

The Victorians loved complicated designs and rich detail. Wickerwork furniture (photo 8) made of rattan, raffia, fruit wood, willow twigs, or other pliable, natural materials lent itself to the decorative taste of the period. In America, the rising

— 6 —

— 7 —

middle classes furnished their newly-built porches and conservatories with rustic and wicker furniture. Today's vinyl coated, aluminum-framed reproductions (photo 9) simulate the look of wicker while remaining unaffected by the weather.

— 8 —

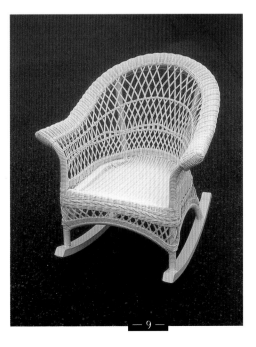

— 9 —

– 10 –

– 11 –

The wheelbarrow bench (photo 10) was a product of the Arts and Crafts movement of the 1880s, which preached an aesthetic of utility and simplicity (compared to the Victorians, that is). Amusing and practical at the same time, the bench reflected the new idea that garden seating could be moved from one part of the garden to another, rather than remaining a permanently-sited fixture.

From the beginning of his career in Edwardian England of the early 1900s, Sir Edwin Lutyens designed and created some of England's finest country homes and gardens. He also designed a garden bench that remains a world famous "classic." The Lutyens bench (photo 11) has an elegant scrolled and latticed back that contrasts beautifully with its long, flat seat and wide bottom rails.

Two other classic wooden seats deserve special note. The steamer chair (photo 12) appeared during the great era of ocean liner travel in the early 20th century. It remains a symbol of leisure in the grand style, and reproduction versions still make

handy poolside seating. On a humbler note, the beloved Adirondack chair (photo 13) remains a classic and also a mystery, because its true origin is unknown. Adirondacks first appeared in the 1920s, and were originally constructed by nailing together pieces of scrap wood. The chair is frequently confused with the older Westport chair, which is similar and definitely originated in the Adirondack Mountain region of upstate New York.

Seating designers have always taken advantage of new materials to create modern classics. The 1930s bench at La Foce in Tuscany, Italy (photo 14) was designed by Cecil Pinsent to reflect classical influences, but it is made of travertine, a type of cast concrete.

Right: Two logs, a simple plank, and exterior house paint were all it took to create this bench. It stands in front of a section of *Laughing Trees*, an outdoor installation by James Malone, Atlanta, GA.

Photo by Janice Eaton Kilby

Far right: Jimmy Straehla, *Transformation*, 2000, 48 x 36 x 28 in. (122 x 91 x 71 cm); antique heart pine, sheet metal, granite, oak tree limbs, copper wire, lath; sawn, screwed.

Photo by Rinne Allen

Lower right: This happy-go-lucky seat is made from old farm equipment, including a tractor seat, wheel, and horseshoes.

Chapter II

Found, Recycled, & Ready-made Objects

I f you're using materials salvaged from dumpsters, demolition sites, tree trimming, junkyards, or your own garage to make your garden seating, good for you! You're doing the planet a favor by not adding to our endless stream of production and consumption. You'll also have all the advantages—and the challenges—presented by the original materials, all mixed together! You'll be inspired to think creatively and to look at the materials you have at hand in a new light.

When working with mixed components, you'll also need to figure out how to attach similar and dissimilar materials. There's an abundance of metal you can recycle into seating, because metal tends to last longer in a scrap heap. Learn to recognize when it's really unnecessary to weld. Drilling pilot holes and bolting or wiring components together are good ways to connect dissimilar objects, or you may be able to stack piece on top of piece and let the existing weight hold everything in place. If you really must weld because the pieces will be load-bearing, make sure you're not trying to weld aluminum (impossible without special materials) or galvanized tin or steel (doing so produces toxic fumes).

You can apply a coat of sealer, if desired, to arrest the oxidation or weathering of your material. Some craftspeople using salvaged material prefer to leave things "just as they are," while others merrily repaint or refinish.

Tools for working with recycled components are as various as the materials themselves, but never shortchange your safety when working with metal. Always wear safety goggles and gloves.

This chair was made from the seat of an old outdoor chair and remnants of antique iron fencing.

CIRCLE YOUR WAGONS

DESIGNER
ROB PULLEYN

Who said we always have to act like grown-ups, especially when it comes to playing outdoors! Why not start collecting little red wagons for fun, easy seating? Wheel them out for spontaneous festivities, add cushions and throw rugs, and everyone's inner child can come out and play in comfort!

MATERIALS

Variety of four-wheeled metal wagons

Assorted cushions and pillows, approximately the same size as wagon interior

Assorted small carpets and rag rugs

Wood shims or blocks

INSTRUCTIONS

1. Arrange the wagons in a circle so your guests can face each other, or in separate conversational groups if you prefer.

2. Fit the cushions into the wagon beds. Cover the cushions with the carpets or rag rugs for extra comfort.

3. To stabilize the wagons and keep them from rolling, tuck the wood shims or blocks between the bottom of the wheels and the ground.

Straw Bale Conversation Couch and Chair

DESIGNERS
Rob Pulleyn & Lisa Mandle

These have to be the easiest seats you'll ever make! Straw bales come in sizes that are perfect for making benches and chairs. The length of a bale can fit two people, and the width is just right for a comfortable seat. After a season of enjoyment, the straw makes great mulch for your garden.

MATERIALS

29 straw bales, each measuring approximately 18 x 24 x 42 inches (45.7 x 61 x 106.68 cm)

4 pieces of rebar, each 3 feet (.9 m) long (optional)

Assorted pillows, throws, and rugs

INSTRUCTIONS

1. The couch shown uses a total of 19 straw bales, and the chair requires 10. Bales can vary in their dimensions, so be open to altering the plan as necessary. The beauty of this construction technique is that you can always change your mind! Referring to fig. 1, arrange six bales side by side, butted against each other, to create the seat. Lay the bottom tier of bales, positioning four bales end to end behind the seat. If you wish, you can stabilize the back further by sinking the three pieces of rebar into the ground along the back of the couch, then impaling the back bales on the rebar. Lay four more bales, end to end and centered on top of the four-bale tier, to complete the back. Lay two more bales, one at each end of the couch, to form the armrests. The back ends of the armrest bales should butt against the bales projecting from each end of the bottom back tier.

2. To construct the chair, refer to fig. 2. Stack four bales on top of each other to form the chair back, then butt the 42-inch (106.68 cm) edges of four bales against each other to form the seat. If desired, you can stabilize the back bales with a piece of rebar. Position one bale on each side to create the armrests.

3. Decorate the couch and chair with the throws, rugs, and pillows as desired for extra comfort. Covering the seats with a long rug is a particularly good idea, so the straw doesn't tickle bare legs!

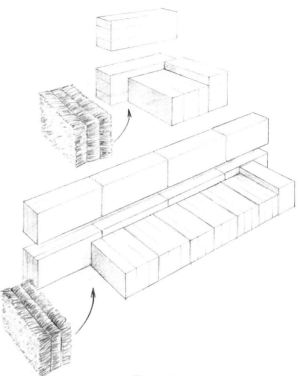

Figure 1

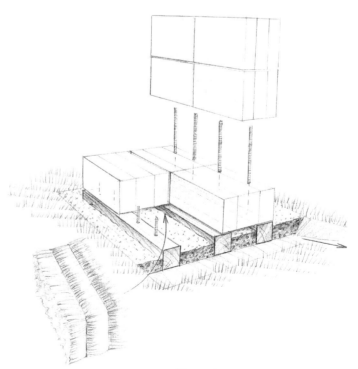

Figure 2

Beauty and the Beast Garden Chair

DESIGNER
Christopher D. Mello

D*o you have a cast-iron chair that's lost its legs, but what's left is still seat-worthy? Try pairing the delicate curlicues of the ironwork with a rough-hewn, sturdy tree trunk. It's easy, and the styles blend together remarkably well.*

MATERIALS AND TOOLS

Top half of cast iron garden chair (legs removed)

Metal file or grinder

Tree trunk, 16 to 18 inches (40.6 to 45.7 cm) high and the same approximate diameter as the chair bottom

Pencil (optional)

Power drill with ⅛-inch (3 mm) drill bit (optional)

Two ¼-inch (6 mm) wood screws, 2 inches (5.1 cm) long

Two ¼-inch (6 mm) washers (optional)

INSTRUCTIONS

1. If there are any protrusions or bits of metal on the chair bottom where the legs used to be, file them off with the file or knock them off with the grinder.

2. Set the chair on top of the tree trunk, positioning it so the chair is balanced and its front edge overhangs the trunk slightly.

3. The weight of the chair should hold it in place, but if you wish, you can secure it to the trunk. To do so, use the pencil to mark two open places between the ironwork where you can sink the screws into the tree trunk. Drill a ⅛-inch (3 mm) pilot hole at both points, then sink the screws through the washers and into the wood to hold the seat in place.

Water-Wise Living Garden Bench
DESIGNER
Christopher D. Mello

*T*hree pieces of "found" industrial metal, plus a gorgeous array of easy-care plants, are all it takes to create this sumptuous bench. No cutting or welding is required. The plants are succulents and fragrant herbs of Mediterranean origin that thrive in heat and drought. The metal collects and releases warmth, something these plants love. Visit junkyards to find unique objects that make this bench all your own, and feel free to modify the directions to use a smaller piece of metal.

MATERIALS

Piece of ½- or ¼-inch (1.3 cm or 6 mm) metal, approximately 2½ feet (76.2 cm) wide and 4 to 5 feet (1.2 to 1.5 m) long, with random holes piercing the material (the one shown in the photo is called a check plate)

Hollow metal pipe, 10 to 12 inches (25.4 to 30.5 cm) in diameter and 16 to 18 inches (40.6 to 45.7 cm) high (the one in the photo is called a pipe clamp)

Metal piece or assemblage 16 to 18 inches high (40.6 to 45.7 cm) (the one in the photo is a gate valve for a sprinkler system)

Additional large-diameter pipes (optional)

Herbs and perennial plants, including: wooly thyme, silver thyme, lemon thyme, common thyme, bronze fennel, lavender provence, weeping hemlocks, sedums, purple sage, lemon grass, and santolina

Annuals, including: purple heart, coleus, euphorbia, porcelain berry, catmint, and black sweet potato vine

Edging stone (optional)

Old manhole covers or metal plates of similar size (optional)

TOOLS AND SUPPLIES

2 x 4 board

Level

Shovel or garden trowel

Potting soil

Garden hose or watering can

Hoe

Rake

Mulch

INSTRUCTIONS

1. Select the site for your bench, and determine where the two ends of the metal seat plate will fall. Position the two metal objects that will serve as the main bench supports approximately 6 to 8 inches (15.2 to 20.3 cm) inside the ends of the plate, with the pipe positioned under one of the openings in the seat plate. If desired, place additional pipes underneath any other openings in the plate. Push them firmly into the ground, and use the board and level to check that their tops are level, adjusting as necessary.

2. Use the shovel or trowel to fill the pipe supports with the potting soil, and moisten with water.

3. Place the metal seat plate on the supports, making sure the plate's openings are over the pipes filled with soil. Check that the seat is firm and doesn't wobble.

4. Plant some of the herbs in the seat by inserting them through the holes in the plate into the soil below. When you sit on the bench and brush or crush the herbs slightly, they'll release wonderful fragrances.

5. Use the hoe and rake to cultivate the soil around the bench, and plant more herbs, perennials, and annuals in arrangements that please you. The smaller, creeping herbs and succulents work best on the ground and under the seat. Plant the taller plants behind and beside the bench to form a living "frame," staggering them so the shorter plants are positioned in front of the taller plants.

6. Sprinkle mulch at the bases of the plants, covering any bare dirt, and edge the seating area with the edging stones, if desired, planting them on end in the ground. Spray lightly with the garden hose.

7. For a nice final touch, you can sink old manhole covers or metal plates into the ground in front of the bench to serve as footrests.

FLYING LAWN CHAIR

DESIGNER
CHRISTOPHER D. MELLO

W hat made you think a lawn chair was only for sitting on a sedate green lawn? With some lengths of chain, you can turn it into a whimsical ornament for a trellis. If you want to sit in your flying lawn chair, do so only if the trellis is constructed to bear the extra weight, the chair's metal is very strong with absolutely no corrosion, and you're confident of the strength of the chain and the welds.

MATERIALS AND TOOLS

Metal lawn chair

Ladder

Tape measure

½-inch (1.3 cm) chain, in a length determined by the height of the supporting trellis

Metal shears

Needle-nose pliers

Welding equipment (optional)

Level

4 double-ended S-hooks, 4 inches (10.2 cm)

INSTRUCTIONS

1. Measure for the length of the chain attachments. Decide how high you want the chair to hang from the trellis, after making sure the trellis is constructed to bear extra weight. Using the tape measure and allowing for the distance the chair will be elevated off the ground, determine the distance from the trellis crosspiece to the sides of the chair immediately beside the armrests. Use the shears to cut two lengths of chain to match that distance, or use the pliers to unlink them.

2. Now, measure from the trellis cross-piece to the sides of the seat bottom, close to the front and beside each armrest. Cut two equivalent lengths of chain.

3. If you've never welded before, take the chair to a welding shop. Weld the first two chains you cut. Weld one end of one of the chains to the chair seat immediately behind the armrest, leaving the other end free. Repeat with the second chain on the other side of the chair seat. Weld the remaining two chains in place, one end on each side of the front edge of the chair seat.

4. Attach the free end of each welded chain to one of the S-hooks.

5. Hang the S-hooks from the trellis. Use the level to make sure the chair seat is hung evenly, adjusting the chain length if necessary. Squeeze the S-hooks closed with the pliers.

Chapter III

Rustic Wood

Rustic materials are abundantly available. With the permission of the property owner, you can cut trees and branches and use them green, or let them dry and then build with them. You can easily collect the leftovers of tree-cutting services or road crews. As a side benefit, you may be performing an environmental service by thinning undergrowth or collecting materials that are considered invasive pests. On the other hand, you can't just drive to a local home improvement center and buy your material in easily quantified, precut dimensions. You have to be prepared to climb, saw, and haul, sometimes from deep in the woods, and the weather can challenge your collecting efforts.

When you collect wood, inspect it carefully for insect holes. If you find any, leave those pieces behind, or you might be importing more damage. You could try heating the wood with a heat lamp to get insects to vacate, but it's preferable to avoid the problem in the first place. Some rustic seating, such as the Wattle-Go-Round Tree Surround on page 42, is built with freshly cut, "green" material to take advantage of its greater pliability. In pieces where pliability is not an issue, you can avoid unantic-

Laura Spector, rustic bench with Balinese temple umbrella, 2000, 58 x 48 x 21 in. (147 x 122 x 53 cm); oriental bittersweet, picket fencing, moss; nailed, screwed

PHOTO BY ENID MUNROE

Before mankind started sawing, planing, or turning wood to create lumber and wooden components, rustic wood was one of our most convenient materials of choice. Rustic construction utilizes found and foraged branches, limbs, and vines in their natural state, with the bark on or off. This type of material therefore has loads of character and individual quirkiness, but it's not appropriate for a seat that requires precision engineering. For example, the form of the oriental bittersweet vine (*Celastrus orbiculatus*) can vary greatly, depending on how it has wound around its host tree.

ipated shrinkage or movement by drying cut 1- to 2-inch (2.5 to 5.1 cm) saplings in a warm, airy place for two to four months before using them.

Rustic construction can be meditative, or relatively fast and free-form, "going with the flow" of the materials and using them as their form dictates. Precision is required only when it comes to making sure the seat is stable and level. There are no real rules to calculating the quantity of materials you'll need, although, depending on its finished size, a seat will require at least four of the largest diameter branches for legs, two for arms, one to three for back supports, four smaller-diameter branches or vines for cross braces, and filler material.

Surface Decoration and Protection

Rustic wood is frequently left unfinished, but you can give it a more finished appearance if you desire. Use sandpaper to remove dirt and burrs and to open up the bark surface slightly. Wearing protective neoprene gloves, brush on a finish coat of one part boiled linseed oil and one part turpentine or mineral spirits, let dry, then apply again. After it's dry, wipe it down with a rag, apply a coat of wax using very fine steel wool, then buff. Bittersweet vine furniture, when treated with a water-repellent wood sealer, can last seven to 10 years, or more. However, rustic furniture is so easy to make and casual in nature, durability may not be an issue for you; it's easy to make more when the useful life of a rustic seat has run its course.

Opposite page, bottom: This rustic chair is made from recycled pickets, salvaged cedar, hardwood saplings, and oriental bittersweet. Janice Shields, Cut It Out, Lenox, MA.

PHOTO BY LINDY SMITH

MATERIALS

Hickory, oak, ash, or laurel sapling wood, 2- to 3-inch (5 to 7.5 cm) diameter, enough to make four 15-inch (38 cm) pieces, two 12-inch pieces (30.5 cm), and one 24-inch (61 cm) piece

Board, 1 x 12 x 24 inches (1.9 x 28.58 cm)

Flexible vine such as bittersweet, grapevine, laurel, or smoke vine, 36 to 40 feet (10.8 to 12 m) total, with diameters ranging from ½ inch to 2 inches (1.3 to 5.1 cm)

Sheet moss sized to cover a 16 x 28-inch (40.6 x 71.1 cm) area

TOOLS AND SUPPLIES

Tape measure

Pencil

Saw

Hammer

Cement-coated nails in assorted lengths, 1 to 4 inches (2.5 to 10.2 cm)

6d finish nails

Rustic Mossy Garden Chair

DESIGNER
Edith Howard for Applewood Crafts

What could possibly fit more naturally into your garden than a chair you've crafted from local wood and vines with the bark left on? Extremely easy to make, this project doesn't require any power tools or extensive weaving. The moss-covered seat lends a luxurious touch of completely natural comfort.

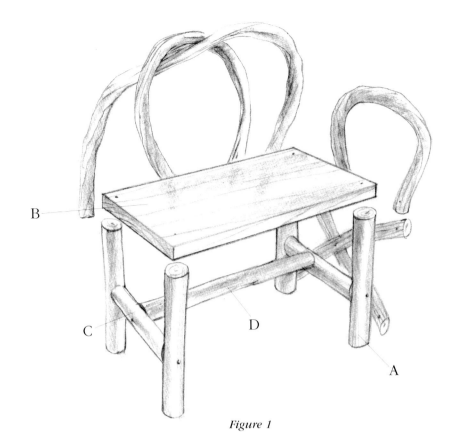

Figure 1

INSTRUCTIONS

1. Use the tape measure and pencil to mark the sapling in four 15-inch (38 cm) lengths, and cut them out with the saw, making sure they're exactly the same length and their ends are flat. These will form the legs (A) of the chair (see fig. 1).

2. Position the legs (A) at the four corners of the board (B), and drive the nails through the top of the board and into one end of each leg. Use two nails to secure each corner.

3. To give the chair extra stability, attach the side braces (C) and center brace (D). First, check the length of the side braces versus the distance available between the front and back legs, and trim the length of each brace just enough so it fits snugly between the two legs. You'll probably trim

between 4 and 8 inches (10.2 and 20.3 cm), but check first. Nail the braces in place.

4. Trim and install the center brace (D) between the two side braces (C), using the same process as step 3. Nail in place.

5. Now you'll make the decorative vine trim. Hold the vine against the chair to determine how long the pieces should be to create the crisscross patterns on the front, back, and sides (for clarity, fig. 1 shows only a crisscross pattern on one side). Make cut marks with the pencil and saw them off as you go. Nail in place.

6. Select large-diameter vines, and bend them into two arcs to form the chair armrests, shaping and twisting as you like. Before cutting, allow an extra 6 to 8 inches (15.2 to 20.3 cm) of length to each

"armrest" vine so that both ends of each armrest will extend below the edges of the chair by 3 or 4 inches (7.6 to 10.2 cm). Nail the armrests to the chair seat and/or legs. Add any additional decorative pieces of vine that appeal to you, intertwining them with the arms, and nail in place.

7. Use the process described in step 6 to create the chair back, twisting and interlocking the pieces as shown in the photograph and fig. 1.

8. Lay the sheet moss on top of the seat, positioning it so it hangs decoratively over the edges. Cut narrow pieces of vine, and attach them to the front and top of the seat with the finish nails to secure the moss to the seat.

MATERIALS

16 wood staves*, each about 2 inches (5 cm) in diameter by 30 inches (76.2 cm) long, for the outer circle

8 wood staves*, each about 2 inches (5 cm) in diameter by 36 inches (91.44 cm) long, for the inner circle

Pliable limbs or shoots from willow, hickory, elm, or cedar in a large enough quantity to weave 26 times around the surround

16 seat supports made from pliable limbs, each about 6 to 7 feet (1.8 to 2.1 m) long

Two 4 x 8-foot (7.2 x 2.4 m) sheets of ½-inch (1.3 cm) exterior-grade plywood

*Hickory or locust wood are good rot-resistant choices.

TOOLS AND SUPPLIES

Ball of string

Scissors

Tape measure

Fine-tip permanent marker

Hammer

Sledgehammer

Nails in assorted sizes, from 1½ to 3 inches (3.8 to 7.6 cm) long

Nail gun (optional)

Pruning saw

Pruning shears or loppers

Jigsaw

Wattle-Go-Round Tree Surround

In the European countryside, you'll often see rustic "wattle" fences woven from stripped limbs and rough branches. This unique tree surround uses the same construction techniques to produce a delightfully rustic surround.

Figure 1

INSTRUCTIONS

1. Select the tree to serve as the focal point of your surround. Surrounds look best with trees that are no smaller than 3 feet (.9 m) in diameter.

2. First, you'll make the outer circle of the surround. The surround shown in the photograph has a diameter of approximately 8 feet (2.4 m) and a 4-foot (1.2m) radius if measured from the center of the tree. Tie the string in a loose loop around the tree, and use the scissors to trim it to the desired radius of the bench. Using the end of the string as a guide, walk slowly around the tree and etch a circle in the

ground with a stick to serve as a guide for the surround.

3. On all 24 staves, make a mark 12 inches (30.5 cm) from the bottom end. Plant the sixteen 30-inch (76.2 cm) staves in the ground, evenly spacing them by eye along the circumference of your etched circle. Sink the staves up to your marks, or 12 inches (30.5 cm) into the ground, by tapping them in with the sledgehammer. You'll leave 18 inches (61 cm) exposed. Check with the measuring tape to ensure that all the staves are the same height aboveground.

4. Starting at the bottom of the staves in the ground, weave the limbs around the staves in an in-and-out pattern to create the wattle. Continue weaving until you reach the top of the staves. Use the hammer and nails to secure the top course, or row, of limbs to the staves.

5. Now you'll create the inner circle with the eight remaining, 36-inch (91.44 cm) staves. Using the string that you used to create the outer circle in step 2, follow the same steps to etch the inner circle. The difference between the outer and inner circles dictates the width of the seating area. The width of the seating area on the bench pictured is about 30 inches (76.2 cm) minus

2 inches (5 cm) to account for the seat's overhang, so make sure to adjust the length of the string accordingly.

6. Position the staves at roughly equal distances around the inner circle, and sink them 12 inches (30.5 cm) into the ground, leaving 24 inches (60.96 cm) exposed.

7. Nail the seat supports to the staves in the pattern shown in fig. 1, flush with the tops of the staves. The inner ends of the seat supports bend and extend up the tree about 18 inches (45.7 cm). Use a pliable limb to belt the support extensions to the tree, as shown in the photograph.

8. Mark the two pieces of plywood with arcs as shown in fig. 2. To make the arc, find the midpoint of the 4-foot (1.2 m) side, and drive in a nail. Tie one end of some string to the nail, then cut the free end to 4 feet (1.2 m) long. Position the marker at the free end, and swing an arc from corner to corner on the plywood to mark the outer radius of the arc. At the midpoint of the outer radius, measure 30 inches (76.2 cm) in from the outer arc (the width of the seat), and repeat the

procedure to create the inner radius of the arc. Repeat the process with the second piece of plywood.

9. Use the jigsaw to cut out the arcs.

10. Lay the plywood arcs on the base of the surround to form a circle, and nail the sheets to the tops of the staves. You'll have an approximately 2-inch (5.1 cm) overhang at the outside perimeter.

11. Cover the seat by nailing branches to the plywood. Follow the circular shape, starting at the outside and working concentrically into the center. Secure the limbs with nails where necessary. When you reach the inner staves, weave the branches in and out of the stave ends, then work your way up to the tops of the staves, or about 6 inches (15.2 cm) high. Finish the seat weaving by nailing a trim of branches around the outer edge of the plywood seat to cover the raw wood.

12. Decorate the back of the bench with branches by nailing them to the seat, then arching them up the trunk of the tree and lapping their ends to create a pleasing design.

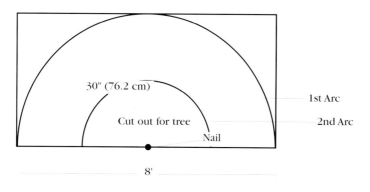

30" (76.2 cm)

Cut out for tree

Nail

1st Arc

2nd Arc

8'

Figure 2

King of Siam Rustic Vine Loveseat

DESIGNER
Laura Spector

You can be emperor or empress of all you survey from this glorious rustic loveseat made of oriental bittersweet vines. The construction technique lends itself very well to improvisation and invention, so relax and have fun while you're making this one-of-a-kind project.

Detail: Braided, twisted, gnarled, corkscrewed, or straight, rustic vines can give effects ranging from romantic, to whimsical, to elegant.

PHOTO BY ENID MUNROE

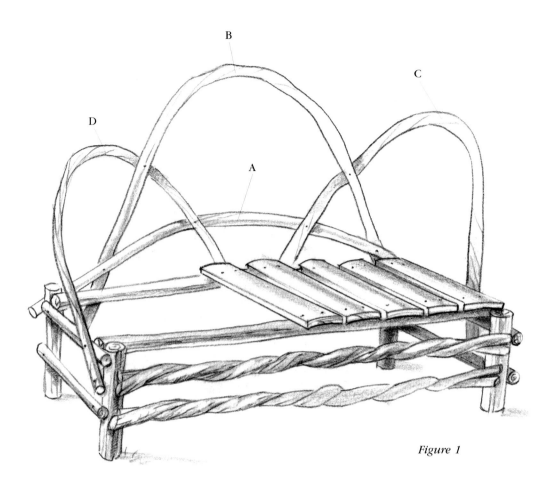

Figure 1

INSTRUCTIONS

1. Use the chalk and ruler to draw two parallel lines 10 inches (25.4 cm) apart on a flat surface, such as a patio. Connect the lines by drawing a perpendicular line 9 inches (22.9 cm) above the bottom of the two lines.

2. Lay one pair of legs on the parallel lines, and one 18-inch (45.7 cm) side rung on the perpendicular line. Secure with the hammer and nails or the power drill and screws. Put aside. Construct a second unit of legs and side rung the same way.

3. Now you'll assemble the base while referring to fig. 1. Stand the leg units up approximately 42 inches (106.68 cm) apart. Place a 45-inch (114.3 cm) decorative vine over the side rung to connect the leg units, and secure with the nails or screws. Connect the back of the leg units with another 45-inch (114.3 cm) decorative vine secured over the side rungs with nails or screws. For extra support, add a third decorative vine to the front and secure it just below each side rung and under the first front rung.

4. To assemble the seat, layer the second set of 18-inch (45.7 cm) side rungs over the front and back rungs; they should measure approximately 12 inches (30.5 cm) up from the ground. Place the seat supports over the two sets of side rungs, and secure with nails or screws. It's preferable to have the front support a bit thicker than the back; this creates an incline from front to back, which makes the seat more comfortable. Screw or nail the picket fencing slats across the seat supports.

5. Install the lower back support (refer to fig. 1) by selecting a sturdy vine the approximate length of the base. Bend the vine (A) slightly to create a gentle arch, and nail or screw it to the back seat support.

6. Now you'll install the back and sides by forming three overlapping arches (B, C, and D in fig. 1). Select the largest vine, one that's sturdy but flexible, and bend it into a high arch (B). Position the highest point of the arch over the centerpoint of the bench back, and secure both ends of the arch to the back seat support. Now you'll brace the center arch by creating two smaller, angled arches (C and D). Wrap one end of C behind the right side of the center arch, and one end of D behind the left side of the center arch.

Secure the ends. Curve the free ends over and around to the left and right sides of the base and secure with nails or screws.

7. The base structure is now finished, and you can fill in and build up the back and sides by weaving vines over, under, around, and through the three back arches. Work from side to side, and step back occasionally to examine your design choices. Don't forget comfort! Use the C-clamps to hold the vines in place so you can check the design before permanently screwing or nailing them in place.

8. Finish the bench with a light sanding. Wipe down with the rag, then brush on at least two coats of water repellent or wood preservative. Let dry.

If you want to peel the bark from rustic wood, cut the wood just after the tree has put out leaves, and peel it within six weeks for ease of removal.

PHOTO BY RICHARD HASSELBERG

MATERIALS

4 vines, 2-inch (5.1 cm) diameter, each 14 inches (35.6 cm) long, for the legs

4 vines, 1-inch (2.5 cm) diameter, each 18 inches (45.7 cm) long, for the side rungs

2 or 3 decorative vines, 2- to 3-inch (5.1 to 7.6 cm) diameter, each 45 inches (114.3 cm) long, for the front rungs

1 decorative vine, 2- to 3-inch (5.1 to 7.6 cm) diameter, 45 inches (114.3 cm) long (or two tree saplings 45 inches [114.3 cm] long), for seat supports

16 picket fencing slats, each 17 inches (43.2 cm) long, for the seat

Assorted widths and lengths of decorative and straight vines to fill in back and arms

TOOLS AND SUPPLIES

Chalk

Ruler

Hammer and 3-inch (7.6 cm) coiled nails, or power drill and 3-inch (7.6 cm) coiled screws

C-clamps

Sandpaper

Rags

Paintbrush

Water repellent or wood preservative

Chapter IV

Living Trees, Plants & Bamboo

Live trees and plants can be part of your outdoor seating projects in several different ways. They can be the integral support for a seat, such as the Lemonade Tree Swing on page 56, or they can form the seat itself, as shown in the Living Tree Armchair on page 52. Plants can add sensory pleasure and decoration, too. Take a look at the live bamboo in the Easy Shade Lean-To on page 160. It's hard to get much more eco-friendly than this!

Working with Trees

You must choose the right tree for your project, and learn how to work with it without harming it. If you're attaching a bench or swing, never wrap ropes or chains around a limb; it can girdle it and kill it. Bolts installed in holes drilled through limbs are much better; the tree grows back and strengthens the connection. Extensive cutting or drilling can cause infection and rot in a tree, so cut conservatively. Living seats obviously love and need the sun and rain, but protect young trees from sunburn by hanging row cover fabric or other semi-shade over them during hot, sunny weather.

Assembly is very free-form, and your only constraint when training trees to grow in a certain direction is not to bend them so much that they break. The life of the trees is the lifespan of the seat, and you'll have the pleasure of watching it change through the seasons.

Living tree chairs are constructed from tree whips, very young bare-root trees that are 6 to 8 feet (1.8 to 2.4 m) tall. You can either grow them yourself, harvest them from the countryside with the landowner's permission, or buy them from a nursery that stocks large, bare-root trees (get advice on climate-appropriate species). Choose flexible trees like willow, alder, or poplar; conifers may be too compact and stiff.

Far right: When this majestic tree reached the end of its life cycle, it was given new life as a comfortable sculptured seat with a water view. Used with permission from Biltmore Estate, Asheville, North Carolina.

Photo by Evan Bracken

Living Decoration

It's fun to grow "living decoration" on your stone, brick, metal, or concrete seating, as long as it's kept moist. When you're building a garden seat, try incorporating components such as cinder block or large, empty pipes that can hold soil, which in turn can sustain living plants. Try filling crevices and joins in stone or brick seating with topsoil enriched with compost, and tuck in moss, baby ferns, creeping herbs, and low-growing flowers such as alyssum, violets, and self-seeding violas to add texture, scent, and color.

You can encourage moss to grow on cool, hard surfaces by painting them with buttermilk. Moss likes to grow in shady places, cracks, and crevices. For a handy moss-starter solution, dissolve one part porcelain clay (found at ceramic supply distributors and craft stores) into three parts water in a jar, shaking it until it's thick and frothy. Combine one part shredded moss and one part liquid fish fertilizer, mix it into the clay/water solution, and apply it to the surface.

Bamboo

To Western eyes, bamboo evokes a natural, low-technology lifestyle. It's available in a remarkable variety of diameters and colors, and creates a refined or appealingly primitive effect depending on size and proportion.

Bamboo is also lightweight and relatively inexpensive. For the same reasons that some gardeners dislike bamboo, other people like it: it grows rapidly and prolifically, and unlike redwoods or tropical hardwoods, it's a sustainable resource that makes very good sense from the ecological standpoint.

Bamboo is beautiful without additional surface decoration, but you can use an exterior-grade stain to enhance its texture or to emphasize a particular color. Weathering changes the color of untreated bamboo from green, to tan, to silver grey. In wet climates, moss and lichen may also grow on the surface, giving a mottled, organic effect. If unprotected, outdoor bamboo seating may weaken after several rainy seasons, so check the strength of the seat before you sit! Scrubbing or pressure-washing twice a year with a nonsudsing mildew remover followed by one or two coats

Left: Split bamboo slats were drilled and threaded onto cable to create this elegant swing. It was made by Retana Bros., Agroindeba, San Jose, Costa Rica.

PHOTO BY SUE AND ADAM TURTLE/TBQ

of water sealer helps bamboo last up to 10 years. For a longer life, store it in a sheltered place. That's easy, since it's light and easily transported. Add a cushion if you'll be using a bamboo seat for extended sitting.

Your success in building with bamboo will depend on your patience in using the tools and construction techniques for a material that doesn't have any right angles. Bamboo stalks, or *culms*, are cylindrical, non-uniform, and slightly curved, but it's those very irregularities that make up its visual appeal. So slow down and enjoy the process! When you calculate how much bamboo you'll need for a project, allow for the diameter and length of each pole, just as you do with lumber. Poles can be purchased individually or in bundles of 25 or more from mail-order suppliers. In tropical to temperate climatic zones, you can harvest it locally, sawing it off at the base.

Below, right: Try incorporating fragrance into your seating design. When you sit down and brush against the scented herbs in the Water-Wise Living Garden Bench, your nose wil enjoy the result!

MATERIALS AND TOOLS

2 living tree trunks

Handsaw (optional)

Utility knife (optional)

Level

1 hardwood or specialty softwood plank, 2 inches (5.1 cm) thick, in a length that allows you to fit it very snugly between the two trees*

Stones with tapered edges

4 metal spikes, 4 to 6 inches (10.2 to 15.2 cm) in length (optional)

Hammer (optional)

*It's essential to use a very hard wood for the plank. Redwood, cedar, or chestnut are suitable.

TREE TRUNK PLANK BENCH

If you have two stately trees in your garden, you can actually encourage them, over time, to hold a simple bench in their grasp. Just bear in mind that you want to cause as little injury to the trees as possible. If you're patient, you can use entirely natural processes to fix the bench in place.

INSTRUCTIONS

1. When trees suffer a wound or are penetrated by a foreign object, or when they encounter an immovable object as they grow, they respond by growing more material to cover and surround the site. The tree on the left in the photograph has produced a "branch collar" that has grown over the end of the bench. (If you don't wish to cut the tree, skip to step 2 at this point.) Use the handsaw to remove a lower limb from the area where you want to locate the bench. Wedge the bench in place, using the level to make sure it's level. The tree will grow to cover both ends of the bench. Be warned, however, that removing a tree limb or causing a wound always makes a tree vulnerable to infection and rot, and so should be minimized. To facilitate healing, any loose bark around the edges of the wound should be trimmed away with a utility knife to make a clean, regular edge. Trees also heal best if a wound is left undressed and open to the air; don't paint it or put tar on it.

2. A better method, which doesn't injure the tree, is to simply wedge the plank between the trees, then wedge the tapered stones snugly into any gaps. The trees will gradually begin to grow around the ends of the planks, and when they begin to take hold, you can remove the stones.

3. If you wish, before you wedge the plank in place, use the hammer to drive the metal spikes into the trees, two on each end, to serve as supports for the plank. The tree will grow around the spikes.

Living Tree Armchair

DESIGNER
Richard Reames

MATERIALS

12 pliable, live tree whips such as willow or poplar, each 5 to 6 feet (1.5 to 1.8 m) tall and ½ inch (1.3 cm) in diameter

1 stake, 5 feet (1.5 m) long

TOOLS AND SUPPLIES

Shovel

Tape measure

Plastic stretch tie tape

7 bamboo stakes, 3 feet (.9 m) long, or scrap wood stakes, 1 inch x ¼ inch (2.5 cm x 6 mm), 3 feet (.9 m) long

Baling wire

Wire cutters

Pliers

Hammer

Grafting knife with straight edge blade

Bleach

Water

Pruning shears

W*hat could possibly be more ecologically friendly than making your garden furniture from living trees? It's true you won't get instant gratification from this project, but you'll have the satisfaction of watching your handiwork grow. You can also have fun telling your friends, "Excuse me, but I have to go water my chair!"*

INSTRUCTIONS

1. Anytime from the fall to the early spring is a good time to plant your chair. To start, use the shovel to dig a hole about 2 feet (.6 m) square and 1 foot (.3 m) deep.

2. Use the tape measure to help you mark four spots inside the hole where you'll position your chair legs. To ensure the finished chair is stable, the legs should be about 1½ feet (.45 m) apart and placed in a square pattern.

3. To create the two front chair legs, plant four of the tree whips where each front leg is located. This will use up eight of the 12 whips. As shown in figure 1, bind them tightly with the plastic stretch tie tape at the point where they emerge from the ground. Eight inches (20.3 cm) above the ground, bind them again.

4. Plant two whips at the position for each rear leg. Plant the whips with the largest diameter on the outside perimeter of the chair, and use the smaller-diameter whips on the inside of the chair. The smaller whips will become the chair's arms.

5. To make a frame for the chair, refer to figure 2 and drive four of the bamboo stakes into the ground. Position them at the outside edges of the legs.

6. To create the front edge of the chair, position one of the bamboo stakes between the front two leg stakes so it functions as a horizontal crosspiece. Cut off a piece of the baling wire with the wire cutters, and use it to wire the crosspiece in place, tightening the wire with the pliers if necessary. The cross-

Figure 1

piece should be behind the two front legs of bundled whips.

7. Bend the whips from the front legs over the crosspiece, arching the whips toward the back legs. Starting with the two inside whips (refer to fig.2), cross them over and under each other to form the chair seat.

8. To make the back edge of the chair, create another crosspiece with a stake, and wire it in place. It's important to note that the whips from the chair seat will be trained underneath the crosspiece (see fig. 2). All of the tree whips should now be at the rear of the chair, behind the rear crosspiece.

9. To bend the whips upward, wire a bamboo stake as a crosspiece to the rear leg stakes, about 4 inches above the lower crosspiece. Thread the whips in front of this (upper) rear crosspiece

to force the whips upward.

10. You'll now create the chair arms by using the inside whips from the bundles of rear leg tree whips. Bend the inside whips toward the front of the chair, and loop them down to the surface of the chair seat. Where the loop touches the seat, use the plastic tie tape to bind it to the whip that's closest to the outside of the chair seat. For extra support, weave the remainder of the whip into the chair seat. Make sure the ends of these whips end up higher in the chair than the arm loop.

11. Adjust the spacing between the whips to achieve an evenly woven pattern to the chair seat. Where whips cross, securely tie them together with the plastic tie tape.

12. To finish the chair back, use the hammer to pound in the 5-foot (1.5 m) stake at the rear of the chair at a point midway between the rear legs. You can weave the whips into a decorative chair back, using the stake for extra support.

13. Finish the chair by using an approach graft to join the whips into a single stem. Refer to fig. 3. Spliced or tongued approach grafts are used when stems have the same diameter, while the inlay approach graft is used when one branch is large and the other one is small. Disinfect the grafting knife with bleach and water, then use it to remove small slices of bark and wood, making matching or interlocking cuts in two limbs. Use the tie tape to bind the two limbs together with the cut surfaces touching. When the trees heal, they'll grow and fuse together. In the spring, this can take as little as two months, but the process slows in fall and winter. To form a stronger chair structure, you can also use approach grafts instead of the plastic ties.

14. Graft the tops over a period of time. Start with just two or three whips, and don't graft on any more until the previous graft has "taken," otherwise you may strip bark all the way around the whip, interrupting sap flow, and the

Figure 3

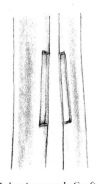
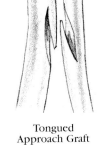

Inlay Approach Graft   Tongued Approach Graft   Spliced Approach Graft

portion above the cut will die back. Decide where you want the top graft to be located, and remove a 5 to 10-inch-long (12.7 to 25.4 cm) strip of bark from each whip. Join and bind the whips with the plastic stretch tie tape. After the graft has grown a ridge of connecting tissue, use the pruning shears to prune away one of the two whips, leaving just enough foliage and buds to ensure one season's growth. After two seasons, prune away the remaining portion of the unwanted whip. Continue to keep an eye on your "lead" whip, pinching back sprouts to help it grow.

15. Keep the chair well-watered during its first summer growing season. When the whips produce side growth, pinch it off. Don't sit in the chair for two or three years until it's grown strong enough to hold your weight.

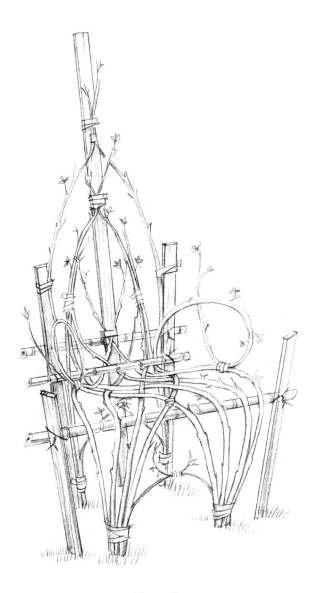

Figure 2

MATERIALS

⅝-inch (1.6 cm) synthetic three-strand rope*

2 galvanized rope thimbles, ⅝ inch (1.6 cm)

2 cast galvanized eye bolts, ⅝ x 14 inches (1.6 x 35.6 cm)

2 flat washers, ⅝ inch (1.6 cm)

4 galvanized nuts, ⅝ inch (1.6 cm)

2 locking washers, ⅝ inch (1.6 cm)

Oak plank, 2 x 10 x 24 inches (can be as long as 42 inches)

*Length depends on tree limb measurement. Avoid manila and cotton ropes, as they tend to decay as they weather.

TOOLS AND SUPPLIES

Ladder

25-foot (7.5 m) metal tape measure

Large nut or bolt (optional)

Ball of cotton string (optional)

Vise (optional)

Vise grips

Crescent wrench

Hammer

Grease pencil or permanent marker

2-cycle gas-powered drill, or ½-inch (1.3 cm) drive electric power drill with a ⅝- or ¹¹⁄₁₆-inch (1.6 cm or 1.7 cm) wood auger bit, 18 inches long (45.7 cm)

Extension cord for electric drill

Safety belt for attachment to tree

Rope for work line

A friend to help you (essential, not optional)

Roll of electrical tape

Utility knife

Level

Lemonade Tree Swing

DESIGNER
Daniel O. Petersen

There's as much art as science to installing a tree swing, and the most important element is picking the right tree to hang it from! Select a substantial hardwood tree if possible. A white oak or live oak is the very best choice. This project also teaches you some important do's and don'ts about installation and safety when working with trees, so you won't harm the tree or hurt yourself in the process. Using both hands for a task while sitting on a limb high above the ground can be risky; always wear a safety belt and use good common sense.

INSTRUCTIONS

1. After you've selected a tree for your swing, look for an appropriate limb. It should branch out perpendicular to the trunk and be a main leader of the tree, 8 to 12 inches (20.3 to 30.5 cm) in diameter and free of decay and hollow areas.

2. Now you'll measure for the rope that will support the swing. Use the ladder to reach the limb if it's not too high, and measure with the tape measure. Double the measurement to allow for the two ropes dropping down from the host limb. With greater heights, tie the nut or bolt to the end of the cotton string, throw it over the limb, and mark the points where the two ends reach the ground. Add 10 feet (3 m) more to allow for doubling the rope at the seat attachment.

3. Swing placement is key to the pleasure of the ride! If there's a slope to the

ground and a good limb running parallel with the level grade, you can install the swing to face the slope's downhill direction, giving the swinger's feet a back stroke close to the ground, and a front stroke that will take him out and high over the falling slope. Make sure the swing is far enough away from the tree trunk to avoid collision, and clear away any obstacles in the swing arc. Be careful: a very long swing can cover an enormous distance, sending you into unforeseen obstacles.

4. The less time you spend up on the tree limb, the better, so do some preparation on the ground before ascending. First, attach the metal rope thimbles to the eyes of the bolts. Clamp a thimble in the vise, or in the vise grips, and bend the thimble apart with the grips or crescent wrench. Slip the thimble around the eye of the bolt, and bend the thimble back into shape, using the wrench or hammer if necessary. Repeat with the second thimble and bolt.

5. Attach the two ends of the rope to the eye bolt. Have the rope ride in the bed of the thimble so that the metal of the thimble rides against the metal of the eye bolt, instead of rope against the metal.

6. As shown in fig. 1, secure the rope to the thimble by braiding it back into itself. Or, you can tie a bowline knot snug to the thimble as shown in fig. 2, leaving enough of a tail to tie a figure eight in the end. This will keep the rope from pulling out.

7. Having secured the two ends of the rope to the thimbles on the eyebolts, place the flat washer, the first nut, the locking washer, and the final nut on each of the eye bolts. This is the order they will go on once the bolts are in the tree.

8. How you attach the swing to the tree is critical to your safety, the swinger's safety, and the tree's continued good health. When you climb up to work on the limb, it's mandatory that you immediately attach yourself to the limb with the safety belt. Never work alone; always have a friend present. Throw the work line over the limb, and use it to haul tools and materials up and down.

9. Use the tape measure and pencil to indicate the placement of two drill holes in the limb. Set the holes at least as far apart as the length of the swing seat; they can be spaced up to twice

Figure 1

that length. (Swings also look better when the space between the ropes at the top narrows to a lesser width at the seat.) Use the power drill with the wood auger bit to drill two plumb holes downward from the top of the limb and through the middle of the limb. Drill the holes through in one smooth continuous motion.

10. Remove the nuts and washers from the eye bolts (to which the ropes are attached). Slip the bolts into the drilled holes from the underside of the limb. Replace the washers and nuts on top, placing the flat washer against the top of the hole, then the first nut, the locking washer, and finally the second nut. Use the crescent wrench to tighten the first nut until the eye end of the bolt on the bottom of the limb and the flat washer on the top side of the limb begin to bite into the limb's bark. Line up the bolt eyes so they face the same direction as the swing arc. After the first nut is tightened, tighten the second nut until the locking washer is flattened between the two nuts. This completes your work in the tree.

11. Now you'll attach the plank seat. The loop of rope hanging from the eye-bolts should be dragging the ground.

Figure 2

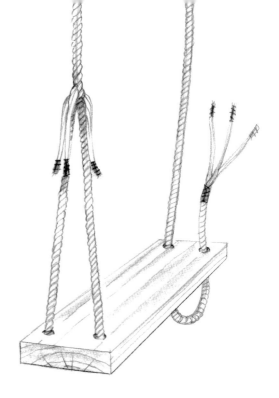

Figure 3

Find the approximate center point of the loop, tape a 3-inch (7.6 cm) section with the electrical tape, and cut through the rope with the knife in the middle of the taped section. Use the tape measure and pencil to mark a drill hole in each corner, 2 inches (5.1 cm) in from the sides and corner. Drill the holes.

12. Thread the newly cut rope ends into the holes in each end of the seat: first down through one hole, then back up through the corresponding hole on the same end. Attach the rope end to the rope coming down from the limb, at a point about 18 inches (45.7 cm) from the seat, using a bowline to create a triangle of rope (see fig. 3). Adjust the seat to a comfortable height, and use the level to check that it's evenly hung, then tape and cut off any excess rope. If desired, braid the ends for a finished look.

Far East Cedar & Bamboo Bench

DESIGNERS
Carol Stangler & Randall Ray

Craftspeople in the Far East know that elegance is often about restraint, and in their work they will often choose to highlight only one or two perfect details. This luxurious bench is a perfect example, with its simple but beautifully finished cedar construction and mitered bamboo inlay.

MATERIALS

10 culms of black bamboo, each 4 to 5 feet (1.2 to 1.5 m) in length

4 x 4 Western red cedar, 8 feet (2.4 m) long

4 x 4 Western red cedar, 10 feet (3 m) long

1 x 2 pressure-treated lumber, 13 feet (3.9 m) total

¾-inch (1.9 cm) pressure-treated plywood, 18 x 24 inches (45.7 cm x 61 cm)

TOOLS AND SUPPLIES

Clear wood sealer

2 bristle paintbrushes

Tape measure

Miter saw

Power drill with ⅜-inch (9.5 mm) and 1⁄16-inch (1.6 mm) bits, a ⅜-inch (9.5 mm) round-over bit

Paste construction adhesive

30 wood screws, 2 inches (5.1 cm) long

Fine sandpaper

Chisel (optional)

Circular saw or table saw

Hammer

Pencil

Wood glue

12 tapered wood plugs

Oil-based wood finish in brown/black shade

Chalk

Bamboo saw*, or hacksaw with a fine-toothed blade for cutting metal

Bamboo splitting knife*

Mallet

Miter box

Box of 1⅝-inch (4.1 cm) ringed panel nails, 1⁄16 inch (1.6 mm) diameter

*Available from mail-order sources for Japanese woodworking tools. A Japanese bamboo saw has a thin blade with 20 to 32 teeth per inch (2.5 cm). The bamboo splitting knife is a froe-type knife with a blade approximately ⅛ inch (3 mm) thick, sharpened to a double bevel.

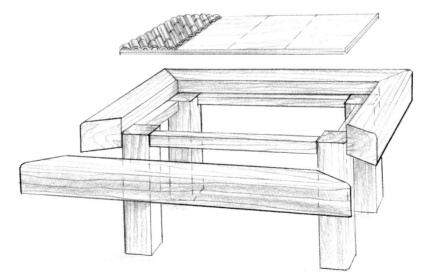

Figure 1

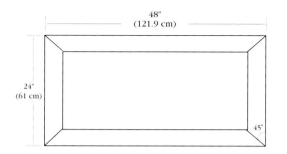

Figure 2

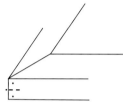

Figure 3

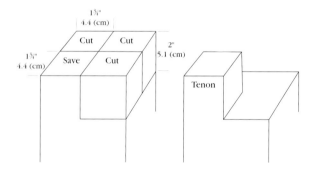

Figure 4

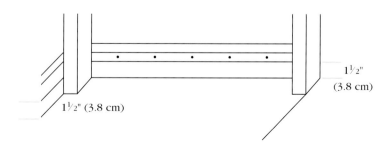

Figure 5

INSTRUCTIONS

1. Wash the bamboo culms and allow them to dry. Paint them with two coats of the clear sealer, following the package directions. Allow to dry.

2. Now you'll make the bench frame. Refer to figures 1 and 2. Measure the two 4 x 4 cedar pieces and cut them to a 45° miter, two with a 48-inch-long (121.92 long point and two with a 24-inch-long (61 cm) point.

3. Assemble the cut cedar pieces on the work surface, and use the ⅜-inch (9.5 mm) drill bit to predrill three ¾-inch-deep (1.9 cm) pilot holes in each corner as shown in figure 3. Use the 1⁄16-inch (1.6 mm) bit to drill an additional 2 inches (5.1 cm) into the center of each hole.

4. Dust off the shavings. Apply the adhesive to the ends of the cut pieces, assemble, and screw them together with the 2-inch (5.1 cm) wood screws, countersinking the screws ⅜ inch (9.5 mm). Allow the adhesive to dry.

5. From the remaining 4 x 4 pieces, square-cut four legs, each 15¾ inches (40 cm) long. Rabbet the top end of each leg, as shown in figure 4. Cut and remove the three sections, leaving a tenon which will fit into the corners of the frame.

6. Place the frame face down, apply the adhesive, and set the tenons into the inside corners of the frame. Drill a 1⁄16-inch (1.6 mm) pilot hole 2 inches (5.1 cm) deep. Screw in the 2-inch (5.1 cm) screws, and let dry. Sand off any excess adhesive, or use the chisel to remove it.

7. Lay the bench on its side, and pencil a line 1½ inches (3.8 cm) below the top edge of the frame (see fig. 5). From the 1 x 2 boards, cut two pieces 37⅝ inches (95.58 cm) long, and two pieces 13¾ inches (34.9 cm) long to serve as cleats.

8. Predrill 1⁄16-inch (1.6 mm) pilot holes every 8 inches (20.3 cm) along the line you've drawn. Position the cleats you cut in step 6 between the legs, along the 1½-inch (3.8 cm) depth line. Screw in place with the 3-inch wood screws.

9. Place the bench upside down. Cut three of the 1 x 2 boards to a 14-inch (35.6 cm) length. Set these stretchers across the width of the bench, between the cleats, as shown in figure 6.

Drill two ¹⁄₁₆-inch (1.6 mm) pilot holes on an angle, then use the 2-inch (5.1 cm) wood screws to toenail the ends of the stretchers onto the cleats.

10. Place the bench upright. Measure and cut the ¾-inch (1.9 cm) plywood to 17 x 41¼ inches (43.2 x 104.78 cm). After applying the wood glue to the top edge of the cleats, center the plywood and drop it into the bench. Secure the plywood to the cleats with the 2-inch (5.1 cm) wood screws, six along each long side, and three along each short side.

11. Use the ⅜-inch (9.5 mm) round-over bit in the drill to router the outside top edge of the frame and the base of the legs, achieving a pleasing curve. Fill the screw holes with the wood plugs.

12. Clean off any dust or shavings, and use the paintbrush to apply two coats of the clear wood sealer to the cedar, following the package directions. Coat the plywood with the brown/black wood stain. Let dry.

13. As shown in figure 7, use the tape measure and chalk to divide the plywood seat into four equal sections.

14. With the bamboo saw, cut the bamboo into ten 16-inch (40.6 cm) lengths. Use the knife and mallet to split the bamboo in half lengthwise, creating 20 pieces. Arrange the halves on the seat in a herringbone pattern (see fig. 8), adjusting them to get a close fit and an even surface. Cut and split the remaining bamboo, and use it to complete the seat's surface pattern.

15. Refer to figure 9. Use the bamboo saw and miter box to miter-cut the ends of the bamboo pieces into complementary 45° angles, where they meet each other at the chalk lines on the seat. Put a straight angle cut on the ends that butt against the seat frame. Work carefully and precisely to achieve a good fit.

16. Lightly sand the cut ends of the bamboo, and stain the ends with the brown/black stain. Allow to dry, then lay the pieces back into the pattern on the seat. Using the ¹⁄₁₆-inch (1.6 mm) drill bit, drill a pilot hole through the end of each bamboo piece and ⅛ inch (3 mm) into the plywood base. Secure by hammering the ringed panel nails through the holes. Each nail should slide through the pilot hole. If the hole is too small, the bamboo will split when you try to hammer in the nail. Drill and nail the ends of each bamboo piece in place until the inlay is complete.

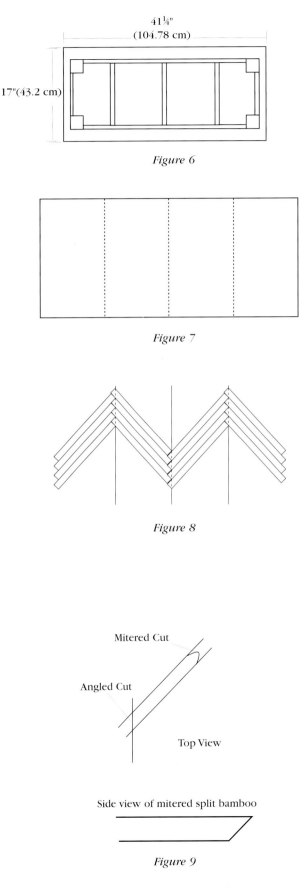

41¼"
(104.78 cm)

17"(43.2 cm)

Figure 6

Figure 7

Figure 8

Mitered Cut

Angled Cut

Top View

Side view of mitered split bamboo

Figure 9

Chapter V

Brick and Stone

Why not use brick as a decorative insert? See the Recycled Brick and Bedstead Bench on page 72.

Brick

You don't have to become a mason to use brick attractively in garden seating. The projects in this book don't require mortar, and you're free to consider other ways to use the material.

Since brick comes in standard dimensions, it's easy to figure out how much you'll need for a project (but check the dimensions with a tape measure). A brick paver usually measures 2 x 3½ x 7¾ inches (5 cm x 8.75 cm x 19.4 cm). To cover a square foot (0.3 sq. m), you'll need about five bricks. So if you want to cover a garden seat that measures 1 x 3 feet (.3 x .9 m), multiply the width by the length, or 1 x 3, to determine the square footage of 3 square feet. You'll therefore need 15 bricks. You can buy new bricks by the piece at home improvement

and building supply centers, brick suppliers, and tile companies. For old bricks, look for architectural recycling stores and demolition sites.

Bricks get hot in the sun and acquire moss in damp climates. Old brick may look absolutely delightful in an outdoor seat, but unless you shelter it, winter weather may cause it to crack or crumble. New brick won't have as much character, but it will last longer.

Stone

When you use stone to make a garden seat, its origin often determines its decorative effect. The larger the stone, the more it blends into the landscape and looks like it just "grew there," as seen in the Floating Stone Slab Bench on page 70. Stone recycled from earlier uses, such as the Recycled Granite Curbing Bench on page 66, has more regular dimensions and a cleaner look.

The advantage of stone is that it lasts almost forever, period. It's impervious to the elements, and if you live in a moist climate, it will probably acquire moss and lichen (if you don't like it, scrub it off with a brush). If you plan to sit long on stone, use a pillow for comfort. Stone's density also means it's very heavy relative to its size, and its main disadvantage is the sheer strength required to lift and move it. Stone work is labor-intensive, so lighten the load by collecting a group of friends to help you!

In many areas of the country, you can simply collect stone from the fields. For very large pieces, go to stone yards, or keep an eye on local road-building projects which may involve blasting and removal of large chunks of stone. Offer to remove some of the debris! If you buy materials at a stone yard, they'll usually deliver. If you move a large piece of stone yourself, you'll need a wheelbarrow, a tire iron or piece of rebar (for leverage), and several pairs of helping hands. In desperate cases, you can rent a pallet jack at a local equipment rental business or home improvement center. If you're working with a stone that weighs more than 200 pounds (90.8 kg), it's advisable to use the services of a professional backhoe operator to move and position it.

Left: Recycled granite curbing was stacked to create this bench.

MATERIALS AND TOOLS

3 pieces of recycled granite curbing, the top piece at least 3 to 5 feet (.9 to 1.5 m) long and the two supporting pieces 16 to 18 inches (41 to 46 cm) long*

Tape measure

Heavy work gloves

Shovel

Level

2 x 4 board

A helpful friend

*These dimensions can vary if you adjust your installation procedure accordingly. See step 2.

RECYCLED GRANITE CURBING BENCH

Y*ou can rest easy on this bench, because you won't get a ticket for parking on the yellow line! An inventive reuse of old curbing torn up in an urban redevelopment project, this project is simple to construct. For opportunities to salvage wonderful pieces of stone to use in your outdoor seating, check with your local road building authorities, and keep your eyes open at demolition sites and architectural renovations.*

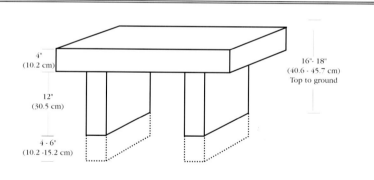

Figure 1

INSTRUCTIONS

1. When choosing materials for a stone bench, it's best to select a top piece that has an even, level top and an even bottom to allow it to make good contact with the supporting stones. This is one reason old street curbing can make good seating, as it's fairly uniform.

2. There are three factors to consider when choosing the length of the two bench supports: the height of the bench, the thickness of the seat, and the depth the supports must sink into the ground. The most comfortable sitting height is 16 to 18 inches (40.6 to 45.7 cm) above the ground. The two pieces that support the bench should sink 4 to 6 inches (10.2 to 15.2 cm) into the ground. You must take this into account along with the actual thickness of the stone that forms the seat (refer to fig. 1). Let's assume you want your

bench to be 16 inches (40.6 cm) tall. Therefore, 16 inches (40.6 cm) minus the 4-inch (10.2 cm) thickness of the bench (you've measured it, right?) equals 12 inches (30.5 cm), and 12 inches (30.5 cm) plus 4 to 6 inches (10.2 to 15.2 cm) (the depth to sink the supports into the ground) equals a supporting stone length of 16 to 18 inches (40.6 to 45.7 cm). If you use slim stones for the bench supports, you'll have to sink them even deeper into the ground for strength and stability, and this will affect your calculations accordingly.

3. When choosing supporting stones of the correct length, try to pick some with flat, even tops so the bench will sit solidly on them.

4. Use the tape measure to determine the length of the bench stone. Wearing your work gloves, sink the two supports into the ground so that the bench will overlap them 6 to 8 inches (15.2 to 20.3 cm) at each end. Refer to fig. 2. For example, if you have a 36-inch-long (91.4 cm) bench and the supports are 4 inches (10.2 cm) thick, subtract

20 inches (50.8 cm). A 6-inch (15.2 cm) overlap plus 4-inch (10.2 cm) thickness equals 10 inches (25.4 cm). Multiply 10 inches (25.4 cm) times two and subtract the result from 36 inches (91.45 cm). There should, therefore, be a 16-inch (40.6 cm) space between the supports. But, having said all that, if your bench stone is noticeably thicker at one end, you can balance the asymmetry by increasing the overlap of the thinner end of the bench stone over its support.

5. Use the level to check that the support tops are even (if you have a small level, set it on the 2 x 4 board balanced on the two supports). Adjust the heights if necessary.

6. With your friend's help, carefully set the bench stone in place on the two supports. Check to make sure it's stable and doesn't rock. If it does, slide the stone slightly over the supports to obtain a flatter contact between them.

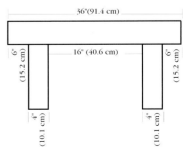

Figure 2

WHEN IS A ROCK NOT A ROCK? MEDITATION BENCH

DESIGNERS
NORMA CHEREN AND TERI STEWART

MATERIALS

Slab of quarried stone or fieldstone, roughly
4 x 19 x 36 inches (10.2 x 48.3 x 91.44 cm)

2 slabs of stone, roughly 2 x 10 x 12 inches
(5.1 x 25.4 x 30.5 cm) or 4 x 12 x 12
(10.2 x 30.5 x 30.5 cm) inches in size

2 or 3 small flat stones

2 cinder blocks, 8 x 8 x 12 inches
(10.2 x 10.2 x 30.5 cm)

TOOLS AND SUPPLIES

Level, at least 12 inches (30.5 cm) long

Shovel

Work gloves

Hammer

2 helpers

Sometimes we do our best thinking when we're alone in our garden. This one-person bench is a wonderful example of how the sensitive choice of materials and their careful placement can transform the humblest elements into an appealing garden seat. And even better, there's no mortar required.

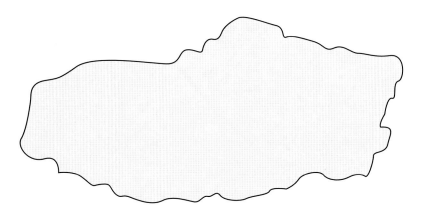

Figure 1

INSTRUCTIONS

1. When selecting the largest slab to serve as the bench seat, the top should be smooth enough to sit on but still have irregularities to make it look more natural and interesting (see fig. 1), and the bottom should be as flat as possible for good contact with the supporting blocks. The two slabs for the sides need to be flat only on one side. The seat slab in the photograph is a schist called Cherokee rock, which is gray with a brilliant mica sheen. The sides are limestone culled from a stoneyard's rubble. The finished bench in the photograph measures 16 x 19 x 36 inches (40.6 x 48.3 x 91.44 cm).

2. Clear a space in your garden that measures approximately 16 x 30 inches (40.6 x 76.2 cm), and use the level to make sure it's not sloped. Tamp down the earth with the shovel, but leave the top inch of soil loose.

3. Wearing your work gloves, set the cinder blocks on their ends, side by side and 4 to 8 inches (10.2 to 20.3 cm) apart, depending on the length and configuration of the slab that will serve as the bench. Work the blocks into the earth until they're firmly in place and their tops are level.

4. With the help of your two assistants, lift the largest slab and place it on the

blocks, moving it to a stable point that's visually attractive.

5. Again with your friends' help, slowly and simultaneously push down the perimeter of the slab, and use the small, flat stones as wedges if necessary, tapping them in with the hammer. The slab should be steady as a rock!

6. Position the smaller slabs flush against the outer faces of the cinder block, the slabs' flat sides against the block. Push the lower end of the slabs firmly into the loose earth.

TOOLS AND MATERIALS

Piece of stone measuring 4 to 5 feet (1.2 to 1.5 m) long, 1½ feet wide (.45 m), and 8 to 10 inches thick (10.2 to 12.7 cm)

3 stones measuring 8 to 12 inches (20.3 to 30.5 cm) long, 8 to 12 inches (20.3 to 30.5 cm) wide, and 4 to 6 inches (10.2 to 15.2 cm) thick

Shovel

Work gloves

Level

2 x 4 board

Motorized backhoe

FLOATING STONE SLAB BENCH

V isitors to your garden will marvel at the way a huge piece of stone forms a bench that appears to "float" over the supports hidden underneath. When you work with stone this size, you'll need a backhoe and the help of someone experienced in running it.

You can choose to make intriguingly stacked stones an integral part of your bench design.

INSTRUCTIONS

1. Stone is extremely heavy relative to its size, and when you're moving a piece that weighs 200 or more pounds (90.8 kg), you'll want to borrow or rent a backhoe to move it. If you don't have experience with this piece of power equipment, enlist the services of an experienced operator. A stone measuring 8 cubic feet (.24 m³) can fall in this weight range, for example. Cubic feet or cubic meters are determined by multiplying length times width times thickness.

2. When choosing the stone for the bench seat, select one with a level top and even bottom. The three pieces of stone will serve as supports, so make sure all three pieces are flat on at least one of the 8- to 12-inch (20.3 to 30.5 cm) edges, so they'll make good contact with the bench. The sitting surface of the bench should be 16 to 18 inches (40.6 to 45.7 cm) above the ground, and the supports should be sunk 4 to 6 inches (10.2 to 15.2 cm) in the ground. Try not to make them any higher, because you want them to be hidden under the bench seat.

3. Use the tape measure to position the three support stones so that the bench will overlap them 6 to 8 inches (15.2 to 20.3 cm) at each end, with the third in the middle. Wearing the work gloves, orient each stone so one of its 8- to 10-inch (20.3 to 25.4 cm) edges runs front to back. Use the shovel to dig holes of the recommended depth, and sink the stones into the ground, packing the earth solidly around them.

4. Use the level on top of the 2 x 4 to check if the support tops are even. Adjust the heights if necessary.

5. Use the backhoe, or have the backhoe operator set the bench stone carefully in place on the three supports. Check to make sure it's stable and doesn't rock. If it does, slide the stone slightly over the supports to obtain a flatter contact.

MATERIALS

9 old bricks

Bed rails

3 scrap metal pieces, the same length as the seat frame

2 pieces of angle iron for the legs, or extra pieces of gate

Old metal gate, 36 to 42 inches (91.4 x 107 cm) wide

Extra decorative metal elements (optional)

TOOLS AND SUPPLIES

Wire brush (optional)

Measuring tape

Safety goggles

Protective gloves

Chalk

Hacksaw

Band saw

Several C-clamps

Welding equipment (optional)

Framing square

Level

Angle grinder

Sanding pad or wire brush (optional)

RECYCLED BRICK AND BEDSTEAD BENCH

DESIGNERS
Johnny and Katina Jones

*T*his *bench design combines modern lines with recycled elements that evoke the past: an old iron gate, a bed frame, and bricks that once paved an early city sidewalk. If you haven't welded before, take the project to a metal fabrication shop to be welded.*

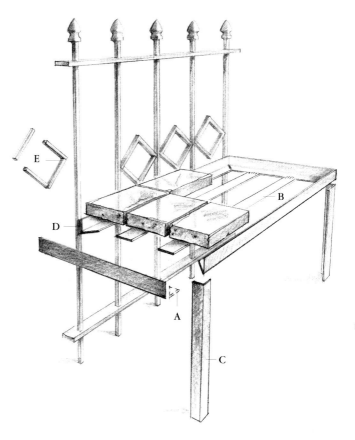

INSTRUCTIONS

1. Place the nine bricks into three rows of three bricks each.

2. Using the tape measure, check the dimensions of the bricks to determine the seat dimensions.

3. You should always wear protection when working with metal, so put on the safety goggles and gloves. Use the chalk to mark the old bed rails to the dimensions of the bricks, and cut with the hacksaw.

4. With the hacksaw or band saw, miter the corners of the rail pieces to form 90° corners for the frame (A) to hold the bricks.

5. Use the C-clamps to clamp the frame pieces to a heatproof work surface. Turn the lips of the angle iron inward so the frame will provide a "ledge" for the bricks along its perimeter. Make sure they're square. Tack, or spot-weld, the frame, or have a weld shop do it for you. Check the corner angles of the frame with the framing square, and make sure the bricks fit inside. Weld the three pieces of scrap metal (B) to the inside of the frame at 3-inch (7.6 cm) intervals, where they'll act as an undersupport to keep the bricks in place.

6. To create the two front legs (C), carefully measure the angle iron to the desired height of the bench, and cut it with the hacksaw. Check that the legs are the same height and level, and even them up with the grinder if necessary. The ideal height of any seat is 16 to 19 inches (40.6 to 48.3 cm) from the ground.

7. Use the angle grinder or sanding pad to clean the tops of the legs. Position the legs flush against the inside front of the seat frame, and weld them in place.

8. Instead of individual legs, you can use extra fencing to serve as legs on the sides of the bench as shown in the photograph. Simply measure pieces of fencing to fit the sides of the seat; in other words, the pieces of fencing should be as long as the seat is deep. Use the hacksaw to cut them to the desired height.

9. Measure the portion of the gate (D) where the seat frame will be attached. The gate serves as the back of the bench.

10. Clamp the frame to the gate, checking to make sure the seat is level.

11. Weld the seat frame to the gate wherever the frame touches the gate, then smooth the welds with the grinder.

12. If desired, weld additional metal decorative elements of your choice (E) to the gate, positioning them inside the spaces between the gate bars.

13. Place the bricks in the seat frame.

Cement

Sherri Warner Hunter, *Garden Throne: A Place to Daydream,* 1999, 65 x 50 x 32 inches (165 x 127 x 81 cm); concrete over polystyrene foam; cut, cemented.

Photo by Evan Bracken

Cement

First, let's clarify our terminology. Cement and concrete are close to being the same thing but not quite. Portland cement is the lime-based powder you buy at the hardware store. When you combine it with water and sand or gravel, you create a mixture that turns into concrete when it hardens. You can also buy cement mix, which contains Portland cement already pre-mixed with sand in bags.

In the construction technique called *ferrocement,* you wrap wire mesh around an inner structure *(armature)* of reinforced metal bar, then pack cement into the form. You can also make ready-made cement seating into something special by applying mosaic; refer to the Botanical Mosaic Garden Bench on page 78.

Cement is messy; wear protective clothing to shield you from the lime's harshness. Site cement projects with care; if you decide to move or replace it, tearing up and removing concrete is quite a chore.

Ferrocement

Ferrocement is a very plastic medium, allowing you to create inventive forms for your seating. It's also inexpensive and extremely durable if the concrete is mixed and cured properly. The forms don't have be extremely precise, but take care to build a good armature, wiring or welding it securely so the form won't sag when you apply the cement. Pack the cement firmly into all the spaces, leaving no voids. You must cure the cement by keeping it wet while its molecules form tight bonds with the wire mesh. The longer it's kept in curing mode, the stronger the bond will be. Hardware stores carry all the tools and materials you'll need.

Painting and Staining Concrete

Don't paint cement unless you're prepared to take it down to the bare surface with a wire brush when you have to repaint it

The fabulous Folk Art Fantasy Bench is a perfect application of the ferrocement construction technique.

With the addition of a couple of pillows, these classical columns are an inventive and attractive use of ready-made concrete forms for seating.

every few years; half-measures don't work. You can always choose to leave it natural or to stain it for lasting color.

To paint concrete, first clean the surface with water and a scrub brush. Let it dry, then degrease and etch the surface by scrubbing it with a mixture of muriatic acid and water, following the package directions. The acid is highly caustic, so work in a well-ventilated area and wear safety glasses and heavy-duty protective rubber gloves. Allow to dry, then apply a base coat of waterproof primer with a brush or roller; the base coat is essential to keep the porous concrete from soaking up the paint. Let dry; apply exterior-grade cement paint, then waterproof sealer.

Interior-exterior concrete stains are available at home improvement centers and hardware stores. New concrete must cure for a minimum of 30 days before staining. You'll have to

This fantastic cement throne is a mosaic *tour de force* utilizing mirror shards and other decorative materials.
PHOTO BY
CHARLES MANN

degrease the concrete, strip off any paint or sealer, and chemically etch the concrete with muriatic acid. Let dry, then apply the stain with a synthetic bristle brush or roller, let dry for 24 hours, then reapply in a direction opposite to the first coat.

Decorating with Tiles and Mosaic

You can decorate seating with mosaics made from stone, glass, mirrors, broken crockery, ceramic tile, and metals by pressing objects into the final coating of cement before it hardens completely.

You can also add mosaic to a cast concrete bench. A pair of tile nippers cuts thin pieces of ceramic or glass tile. Glass cutters and running pliers are also helpful for cutting mirror and glass. Use cyanoacrylate glue or clear silicone adhesive to adhere the bits to the surface, then apply grout to the crevices using a spatula, trowel, or a tool called a float. Grout comes in various colors, or you can tint it yourself with acrylic paint. After the grout dries for 48 to 72 hours, seal the surface with two coats of clear acrylic sealer. Tools and materials are available at craft stores, hardware stores, and home supply centers.

Above: Warm tones of concrete stain are used very effectively in this outdoor banquette. Steven J. Young, ASLA, SJYDesign, Oakland, CA.

PHOTO BY MICHELLE BURKE

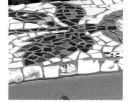

BOTANICAL MOSAIC GARDEN BENCH

DESIGNER
TERRY TAYLOR

MATERIALS

15 to 20 ceramic plates and saucers in white, solid greens, and patterned greens, including one plate with a central botanical motif

Concrete garden bench with removeable top

TOOLS AND SUPPLIES

Safety glasses

Tile nippers

Several polystryrene foam meat trays, or similar containers

2 scraps of 2 x 4 lumber, each approximately 3 feet (90 cm) long

Tape measure

Template on page 80

Scissors

Pencil

Fine-tip permanent marker

Thin-set cement mortar

Mixing container for mortar

Water

Notched trowel

Gray sanded grout

Mixing container for grout

Grout spreader or polyethylene foam wrap*

Palette knife

Sponge

Lint-free rags

*These are the foam sheets used to wrap items being shipped.

*W*hen you look at this gorgeous mosaic bench, you can almost imagine yourself in the garden of a Roman villa.
Give yourself plenty of leisure time to ponder and assemble the mosaic design, so the artist inside you can come out!
You can find all the ceramic pieces you need at thrift stores and yard sales.

INSTRUCTIONS

1. Broken ceramics can be sharp, so always wear your safety glasses when you work. Prepare a supply of shards for the mosaic by using the tile nippers to break the plates in half. Remove the rims from the plates, and trim the rim shards into rectangular pieces 1 to 1½ inches (2.5 to 3.8 cm) wide. Set the rim shards that contain a portion of the plate's finished edge in one of the meat trays. Break the flat portions of the plates into 1 to 2-inch (2.5 to 5.1 cm) pieces that are fairly uniform in thickness, and place them in another tray. It's helpful to keep colors separate. Discard the raised "feet" of the plates and any other pieces that are thicker than the rest.

2. Now, trim the plate with the central motif, making it into a circular tile. Use the tile nippers to carefully remove a small portion of the plate rim. Work toward the raised foot of the plate, removing the rim as you work. Trim the rims as you did in step 1 and set aside. Usingthe tip of the tile nippers, break away a small part of the raised foot. As you work, you'll be able to place the tip of the nippers on the inside of the foot and trim away the foot, leaving a circular, flat plate bottom.

3. Place the scrap lumber under the bench top to elevate it off the floor or ground, so the top will be easier to move when you're finished.

4. Use the tape measure to check the measurements of the bench top.

5. Photocopy the vine template on page 80 and have the copy enlarged to fit the bench you have purchased. Cut out the pattern with the scissors.

6. Center the flat, circular tile that you created in step 2 on the bench top. Use the pencil to sketch a larger circle around the tile as a border area. Place the vine pattern on the bench, and trace around the pattern with a pencil. Flip the pattern over to the other side of the circular tile and trace it again. If you're satisfied with the placement of the central motif and vine pattern, trace over the pencil lines with the permanent marker.

7. In the mixing container, mix a small amount of the thin-set mortar with water according to the manufacturer's instructions.

8. Use the small, notched trowel to spread the mortar on the circular area you sketched on the bench top for your central motif. Position the circular plate bottom in the mortar, and use the plate rims to accent the border area. Use the tip of the trowel to remove any excess mortar that may have squeezed up between the tiles.

9. Working in one small area at a time, spread the mortar around the top edge of the bench. Use the finished plate rims you made in step 1 to create a finished edge of mosaic on the bench top.

10. Start filling in the vine pattern with the solid-colored shards. Spread a small amount of mortar in an area, and use small shards to fill in the vine and leaf shapes, trimming pieces with the tile nipper as needed. Be sure to keep the design lively by varying your placement of colors. Don't try to make the vine pattern absolutely symmetrical and evenly colored; small variations and irregularities add to the charm of the piece.

11. As you work, fill in the small areas between the leaves and vine with white shards. If you have excess mortar in these spaces, fill them in with white shards before the mortar dries.

12. Spread the mortar on the uncovered areas of the bench, and continue filling in with shards. Placing white close to the vine pattern will give the color extra sparkle, but you don't have to make the background completely white. It will be more interesting if you sparingly add bits of green and patterned shards.

13. Allow the mosaic to dry overnight before grouting.

14. Mix the gray sanded grout in the container according to the manufacturer's instructions.

15. Use the grout spreader or the polyethylene foam wrap to spread the grout over the surface of the mosaic. Use pressure to force the grout into all the spaces between the shards. After allowing the grout to set up for about 15 minutes, begin removing the excess grout with the polyethylene foam wrap or rags. Follow the manufacturer's recommendations on the grout packaging for removing any grout "haze" that develops.

16. Allow the mosaic to cure according to the grout's package directions before placing the bench in your garden.

17. Freezing water can cause mosaic to crack, so you'll want to protect your bench from moisture during the winter. Cover it with plastic sheeting, or store it in a sheltered location.

FOLK ART
FANTASY BENCH

DESIGNER
ROBERT CHEATHAM

*With shapes and swirls
inspired by Art Nouveau,
this garden bench sits
squarely in the folk art
tradition of making
fantastic outdoor
constructions with cement,
chicken wire, and paint.
You'll have fun deciding
exactly where you want
the vinelike tendrils
to grow in
your own bench.*

INSTRUCTIONS

1. First you'll make the bench "feet."
Use the metal shears or wire cutters to
cut out four pieces of chicken wire. Cut
the pieces big enough so that when a
piece is wrapped around the end of a 4-
foot (1.2 m) rebar and the rebar is
inserted into a glass vessel, 3 or 4 inches (7.6 or 10.2 cm) of the chicken wire
will stick out of the vessel. Wrap a piece
of chicken wire around one end of each
piece of 4-foot (1.2 m) rebar.

MATERIALS

50-foot (15 m) roll of chicken wire, 2 feet (.6 m) wide with 1-inch (2.5 cm) mesh size

10 pieces of ⅜-inch (9.5 mm) steel rebar, each 4 feet (1.2 m) long

4 glass or porcelain forms, such as screw-on glass light covers, lamp bodies, or other hollow vessel shapes

2 60-pound bags of sand mix cement

Water

5 pieces of ⅜-inch (9.5 mm) steel rebar, each 18 inches (45.7 cm) long

Roll of rebar tie wire

1 can each outdoor-grade epoxy spray paints in red, blue, and green

TOOLS AND SUPPLIES

Metal shears

Wire cutters

Hacksaw

Table vise for making bends in rebar (you can also use a trailer hitch with the ball removed, or a fork in a nearby tree)

Needle-nose pliers

10-gallon plastic bucket

Shovel

Hammer

Heavy-duty protective rubber gloves*

Cement trowel

Garden hose with spray attachment, or plastic mister bottle

Rags or burlap (optional)

*Rubberized fabric gloves are available in hardware stores. They offer the best protection against the sharp ends of the wire mesh.

2. Refer to fig. 1. Using the bucket and shovel, mix water with the cement to pouring consistency according to package directions, making only enough to fill all four vessels. Before it has time to set, pour the cement into each vessel, lightly tapping the sides of the glass to settle any air pockets. Set the vessels in an upright position with the pieces of rebar pointing up, and allow them to dry for three days. With the hammer, rap the glass of the vessels hard enough to break away and remove the glass or porcelain shells.

3. Now you'll start to form the bench frame with two of the "feet." Insert the rebar protruding from a "foot" into the vise, roughly 18 inches (45.7 cm) from the bottom of the foot. Make a bend. Repeat with the second foot. The bends will not be exact 90° angles but will have more of a curve to them (see fig. 2). Position the two front feet in front of the back two feet. Point the bent front pieces back toward the two upright pieces of rebar protruding from the back feet. Allow a 16- to 18-inch (40.6 to 45.7 cm) span to help form the seat, then make a second bend in both pieces of "front feet" rebar so the rods point upward. They will help form the back of the bench.

4. Refer to fig. 2. Place a 4-foot (1.2 m) piece of rebar horizontally across the two front pieces of rebar, an inch or two below the point where the two front pieces start to curve backward. Cut pieces of the tie wire with the

Figure 1

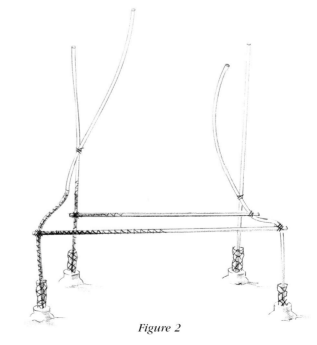

Figure 2

wire cutters, and wire the bar firmly in place on both ends. Do the same with another 4-foot (1.2 m) crosspiece in the back.

5. Using the remaining 4-foot (1.2 m) sections of rebar, fill in the framework of the seat and back with vinelike "tendrils" of rebar as shown in fig. 3, bending and curving them. Connect them with the tie wire to the front and back pieces of horizontal rebar. To temporarily prevent the upper ends of the "tendrils" from falling over, lightly wire them in place.

6. Wire the 18-inch (45.7 cm) sections of rebar in between the bent, 4-foot (1.2 m) sections to fill in the seating area.

7. Use the shears to cut the chicken wire into narrow, 10- to 12-inch (25.4 to 30.5 cm) lengths, and start tightly wrapping the cut mesh around the rebar form. Put on the protective gloves to protect against the sharp ends of the mesh. As you wrap, the mesh should closely follow the desired contours, and in structural and weight-bearing areas like legs and joints, attach at least six layers of mesh for strength. Use the needle-nose pliers or short bits of the tie wire to pull the mesh close in to the rebar. You can also use the shears to cut and fold the chicken wire.

8. When you've wrapped the form with the chickenwire to the desired shape and thickness, apply the cement. A mix of cement the consistency of toothpaste is needed so it will adhere to the wire. Wearing the protective gloves, apply the cement with the trowel and your hands, making sure to press the cement all the way into and around the rebar so there are no gaps or air pockets (see fig. 4).

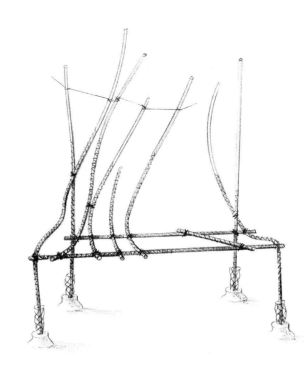

Figure 3

Work as fast as you can so you can apply all the cement in one session. After about an hour, the cement will be set up enough so you can smooth the surface.

9. Using the spray attachment on the garden hose or the mister bottle, mist the cement until it's sopping wet. It's extremely important to keep the bench in the curing stage by hosing it down or misting it every four hours. Keep the bench wet for at least 24 hours and for up to four days. To maintain wetness overnight, saturate the rags or burlap with water and lay them over the bench. Continue to mist the piece periodically. The longer you can keep the bench in curing mode, the stronger the bond will be between the steel and cement.

10. After the bench has cured for 24 hours, mix and apply another coat of cement, if desired, to smooth out the

surface and fill any voids where the cement has dropped out. Let it set up, then mist it and resume the curing process.

11. After the cement has cured and fully dried, spray-paint the bench with outdoor-quality epoxy spray paint. To achieve the look shown in the photograph, apply red to the feet, blue to the legs and the perimeter of the seat, and green to the seat, arms, and back "vines." At the margin of each color, use a delicate touch with the spray paint, blending each tone into the next one without harsh borders.

Figure 4

WOOD

Building with Wood

Lumber is one of our most popular and versatile materials for creating garden seating. With the proper tools, you can cut and shape wood into just about any form you can conceive. You can stain or paint it any color you like, opening up the range of decorative possibilities dramatically. As a material, wood is very strong relative to its weight, and it just plain feels good when you sit in it.

Right: A minimal surface finish complements the gentle arc of the back and simple slat design of this bench.

The main disadvantage of wooden outdoor seating is the lengths to which you have to go to protect it against the effects of being outdoors in the first place! You can buy expensive, extremely durable hardwoods, such as plantation-grown teak, to make your project, or use less expensive pressure-treated (PT) softwood lumber, which has been treated with chemicals to make it last up to 10 times longer than untreated lumber. Some PT lumber is also treated so it can tolerate direct ground contact. When you cut PT, wear gloves and a respirator to avoid the chemicals, and seal it

with a finishing coat. A third option is to use specialty softwoods, such as cypress, cedar, or redwood, which are naturally weather-resistant. Some consumers avoid redwood, not wishing to contribute to forestry pressures on diminishing native American redwood forests.

Sealing, Staining, and Painting Wood

Sun and water can cause wood to turn gray, crack, or rot. A protective layer of paint, stain, clear finish, or water sealer extends wood's longevity dramatically, and a yearly application of water-repellent sealer with a UV filter helps hardwood or specialty softwood outdoor furniture last for decades. If you're scrupulous about maintaining the sealed or painted finish, softwood will last almost as long. Before applying finish, sand the wood to a smooth finish, then remove any dust with a tack cloth. Brush the finish on the clean, dry surface, adding extra coats as recommended.

If you want to show off the grain of hardwood or a specialty softwood and protect it from cracking, apply a coat of penetrating finish water sealer. It doesn't color the wood, though the wood may darken slightly. To further protect decay-resistant redwood and cedar furniture, apply a water repellent with UV protectors and a mildew inhibitor; reapply annually.

Wood stains come in many colors, finishes, and degrees of opacity. For outdoor seating, choose a penetrating stain that also contains a water sealer. A penetrating oil stain soaks in, dyeing wood while allowing the grain to show; it penetrates softwood poorly, however. A pigmented oil stain is handy for changing or matching wood colors, but it can obscure the grain. Water stain is clear and dyes the wood permanently, but it's slow-drying and hard to apply. Re-stain wood every three to five years.

**Below:
Untreated cedar or teak will weather to a silvery gray with time.**

**Below left:
Regular maintenance of painted surfaces is a necessity for wooden outdoor furniture.**

Left: If you choose, you can allow your outdoor furniture to collect moss and lichen so you can enjoy its varied colors and textures.

PHOTO BY RICHARD HASSELBERG

Far right: The weathered and oxidized surfaces of old garden furniture can be beautiful just as they are.

Right: Plant your seat! If you have a seat that's so decrepit it's no longer useful as a seat, try giving it new life as a plant stand or a decorative item in its own right.

Paint covers up flaws and allows you to be creative with color. Use only exterior-grade paint. Oil-based enamel dries slowly, but it's durable, washable, and provides slightly better coverage than latex enamel. Latex is easy to thin and clean up with water. Apply a primer first to seal the wood and help the paint "grab" the surface. Let dry, then brush on the paint.

Why Bother? The Beauty of the Old, the Unfinished, and the Weathered

In some cases you may not want to finish or refinish a piece of outdoor furniture. Hardwoods such as teak, or specialty softwoods such as cedar, will eventually weather to a lovely silvery gray, and this might be all the finish you want for your outdoor seat. You'll have to make the decision whether to allow the weathering and aging process to proceed, or if you want to retard it with sealer, stain, or paint so the material will last longer.

If you're lucky enough to inherit or acquire an old wood (or wicker, or metal) outdoor seat, stop for a moment to appreciate its appeal. The nicks, chips, cracks, marks of wear, and layered surfaces of paint are visual testimony to the passage of time, to the history of the particular piece of furniture, and to the lives of the people who loved and used it before you. The Japanese have a special word, *sabi*, for the patina of age. It's history and poetry combined in an object, to be cherished and not necessarily refinished.

You can "distress" wooden furniture to make it look as if it's been around a long time. Use sloppy, mottled applications of paint in muted tones, and sand selected edges and points to simulate wear. You can also literally batter the furniture with chains (ouch!), brush a contrasting paint or stain over the surface, and quickly wipe most of it off with a rag to leave an "aged" residue in the crevices and depressions. Finally, if a seat has truly outworn its usefulness as a seat, it can make a lovely plant stand in the garden.

Octagonal Tree Surround

*This inviting tree surround is made of eight modular units put together
to form a complete circle. It has very subtle, attractive details such as a comfortably slanted
seat back and bevelled legs. You can make it bigger, or use only a few
of the units if you want something smaller. You'll be most comfortable
making this bench if you have a good grasp of basic carpentry skills,
or if you can work with a friend who does, so
you can achieve the precise cuts and measurements that are needed.*

INSTRUCTIONS

Sizing the Surround

This tree surround is sized for a tree no
larger than 3 feet (.9 m) in diameter,
and it allows for 6 inches (15.2 cm)
between the back of the bench and the
tree. The inside and outside edges of
the surround form two concentric circles that are 22¾ inches (57.8 cm)
apart. If your tree is larger, you'll need
to increase the overall width of each
respective seating unit.

Cutting Out the Parts

1. Cut out all the parts to size. The
part sizing is self-explanatory, with the
following exceptions:

a) Use the circular saw and jigsaw to
cut the back legs (B) to the profile
shown in fig. 1.

b) Both seat rails (E and F) have a
22½° bevel on each end. The bevels
face each other and are cut from the
outer, or "show," face of the board.

c) Both of the back rails (H and I) have
a 22½° bevel on each end, and a 5°
angle on each end on the face side.
This is known as a compound angle.
Carefully lay out the cutline as shown
in fig. 3 on page 92, then use the circular saw tilted to the correct angle to
make the cut.

d) The bottom leg rails (D) are
designed to be cut from a 2 x 6 ripped
into two pieces, each 2½ inches
(6.4 cm) wide. Make the cuts with the
rip guide on the circular saw, or on the
table saw.

e) The seat slats all have 22½° angles,
relative to the face side, on each end (see
fig. 4 on page 93). Use the rafter angle
square to determine the miter cuts, then
saw the angles with the circular saw.

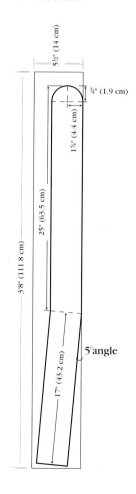

5½" (14 cm)

¾" (1.9 cm)

1¾" (4.4 cm)

25" (63.5 cm)

38" (111.8 cm)

17" (43.2 cm)

5° angle

Figure 1

2. Once you've cut out all the parts, use 150-grit sandpaper and the palm or random-orbit sander to sand all faces, edges, and ends. Be sure to sand the sawn edges of the back legs (B) and the seat slats until they're smooth.

Assembly Notes

Before starting, review the illustration and orientation of the parts. If you're making a complete surround, finish one step of the assembly for all eight

units before you move to the next step. This helps avoid confusion, and it's good practice in any multi-part wood-working project.

Building the Leg Assemblies

1. Lay one front leg (A) and one back leg (B) on a bench or work surface. On the inside edge of each leg, measure 5 inches (12.7 cm) up from the bottom, and square a mark across the edge to

indicate the location of the top edge of the bottom leg rail (D). Refer to fig. 2.

2. Place the bottom leg rail (D) between the two legs (A and B), with its top edge on the marks you made. Place the top leg rail (C) with its top edge even with the top end of the front leg (A) and even with the angle change on the back leg (B); refer to fig. 2. Clamp the two rails between the legs, making sure the faces of all parts are flush.

MATERIALS*

Western red cedar is recommended, or the more expensive hardwoods such as teak or Honduras mahogany, which are harder and rot-resistant.

8 linear feet	2 x 4 x 14 stock
8 linear feet	2 x 6 x 10 stock
7 linear feet	5⁄4 x 6 x 12 stock
4 linear feet	1 x 4 x 8 stock

*The material listed is for building one modular unit.

TOOLS

- Circular saw with a rip guide
- Table saw (optional)
- Jigsaw
- Palm or random-orbit sander
- Rafter angle square (speed square)
- Tape measure
- Bar-style clamps in assorted lengths from 30 to 36 inches (76.2 to 91.44 cm)
- Scrap wood blocks
- 3⁄8-inch (9.5 mm) power drill with 1⁄16 and 3⁄32-inch (1.6 mm and 2.4 mm) drill bits
- Nail set
- A helpful friend

HARDWARE AND SUPPLIES*

- 150-grit sandpaper
- 5 lb. 12d ring-shank common nails
- 1 lb. 6d finish nails
- 3 lb. 8d spiral-shank siding nails
- ½ lb. #8 x 2½-inch wood screws
- Water sealer (optional)
- Paintbrush (optional)

*The hardware listed are for building one modular unit.

CUTTING LIST

The parts listed are for one modular unit. You'll need eight units to construct the entire surround. The dimensions are based on the unit size shown in the illustrations.

Code	Description	Qty.	Material and Dimensions
A	Front legs	2	2 x 4 x 17" (43.2 cm)
B	Back legs	2	2 x 6 x 44"(111.76 cm) cut to shape
C	Top leg rail	2	2 x 4 x 15 7⁄8"(40.3 cm)
D	Bottom leg rail	2	2 x 6, each 2 x 2½ x 15 7⁄8"(40.3 cm)
E	Front seat rail*	1	2 x 4 x 32 ¾"(83.2 cm)
F	Rear seat rail*	1	2 x 4 x 17¼" (43.8cm)
G	Mid seat rail	1	2 x 4 x 17⅛" (43.5 cm)
H	Bottom back rail	1	2 x 4 x 18" (45.7 cm) (refer to illus.)
I	Top back rail	1	2 x 4 x 15" (38.1 cm) (refer to illus.)
J	Back Slats	3	1 x 4 x 13" (33 cm)
Seat Slats*		#1	5⁄4 x 6 x 37"(94 cm)
		#2	5⁄4 x 6 x 32⅛" (81.6 cm)
		#3	5⁄4 x 6 x 27⅜" (69.5 cm)
		#4	5⁄4 x 6 x 22½" (57.2 cm)

*All dimensions are from the long point to long point of a 22½° angle.

3. Drill two ¹⁄₁₆-inch (1.6 mm) pilot holes for 12d ring-shank nails at each joint. Drill through the top and bottom edge of each rail, angling the bit towards the leg. Then toe-nail each leg rail (C and D) into both legs (A and B) by hammering 12d ring-shank nails at an angle through the rails and into the legs. Once you've driven in all the nails, use the nail set to set the heads just below the surface. Remove the clamps and set the assembly aside.

4. Repeat steps 1 through 3 to build the second leg assembly.

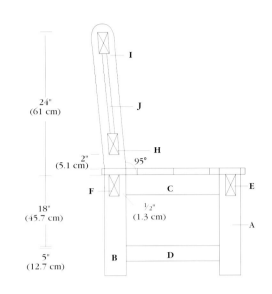

Figure 2

Joining the Leg Assemblies

1. Lay one leg assembly, with its inside face up, on a bench. On the front leg (A), make a mark ½ inch (1.3 cm) in from the front edge at the top of the leg. Make another mark ½ inch (1.3 cm) in from the front edge, 3 inches (7.6 cm) down from the top end.

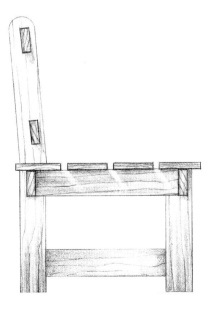

2. On the back leg (B), square a line across the inside face at the top edge of the top seat rail (C). Then, make marks ½ inch (1.3 cm) in from the back edge of the back leg (B) on this first line, and another line 3 inches (7.6 cm) down from this line.

3. Repeat steps 1 and 2 with the other leg assembly. These marks will locate the front and rear seat rails (E and F), which you'll now install.

4. Find a friend to help you at this point. Stand the two leg assemblies upright with their inside faces toward each other. Place the front leg rail (E) between the front legs (A) of the leg assembly, with its top edge even with the top ends of the legs and its face side on the two marks you made in step 1. Place a clamp across the setup to hold the seat rail in place.

5. Place the rear seat rail (F) between the back legs (B) of the leg assembly, with the top edge and the rear face of

the rail even with the marks you made in step 2. Clamp the rail to the legs, using wood scraps if necessary to prevent marring the legs. Check to see that both seat rails (E and F) are aligned with each other.

6. Drill two ¹⁄₁₆-inch (1.6 mm) pilot holes for 12d ring-shank nails from the outside face of one front leg (A) into the beveled end of the front seat rail (E). Center the pilot holes relative to the width of the seat rail. Repeat this procedure for the other front leg (A) and front seat rail (E). Then use the same procedure to drill pairs of pilot holes from the outside face of the back legs (B) and into the rear seat rail (F). Secure the joints by hammering 12d nails into all the pilot holes you just made. Set all the nail heads with a nail set, then remove the clamps.

7. On the inside face of the front seat rail (E), mark the center, then make a mark ¾ inch (1.9 cm) on either side of your center mark. Square the two outer marks across the face of the rail so you have two lines 1½ inches (3.8 cm) apart centered lengthwise on this rail. Repeat this procedure to create two lines 1½ inches (3.8 cm) apart and centered lengthwise on the inside face on the rear seat rail (F).

8. Place the mid seat rail (G) between the front (E) and rear (F) seat rails, centered on the marks you made on the rails in step 7. Refer to fig. 3. Clamp in place.

9. Drill two ¹⁄₁₆-inch (1.6 mm) pilot holes for 12d nails from the outside face of the front seat rail (E) and the outside face of the rear seat rail (F), into the end of the mid seat rail (G). Secure the mid seat rail by hammering one 12d nail through each pilot hole you just made. Remove the clamp and check all connections to make sure they're tight.

Adding the Seat

1. Position seat slat #1 on top of the seat rails of the leg assembly. The front edge of the slat should extend approximately 1 inch (2.5 cm) past the face of the front seat rail (E), and both mitered ends should be flush with the outside face of the two top leg rails (C). Clamp the slat in place.

2. Place the remaining seat slats (#2, 3, and 4) on top of the seat rails. Maintain a ¼-inch (6 mm) gap between each slat, and be sure that the slat ends are flush with the outside face of both top leg rails (C). Use ¼-inch-thick (6 mm) scrap spacer blocks between the slats if necessary to help achieve even gaps. Mark seat slat #4 for the notches required to fit it around the two back legs (B), as shown in fig. 4. Cut the notches with the jigsaw.

3. Drill two ³⁄₃₂-inch (.024 mm) pilot holes for 8d spiral-shank siding nails at each end of each seat slat into the top leg rails, and two pilot holes into the mid seat rail (G). Keep the pilot holes ¾ inch (1.9 cm) away from the edges and ends to prevent splitting. Hammer one 8d nail through each pilot hole to secure each seat slat to the top leg rails (C) and mid seat rail (G). Remove any clamps used to hold down the slats.

Attaching the Back

1. To locate the bottom and top back rails (H and I), make the following marks on the inside face of each back leg (B):

For the bottom back rail (H), measure up 2 inches (5.1 cm) from the top of seat slat #4, and square a line across the inside face. Then measure in 1/2 inch (1.3 cm) from the front edge, make a mark on the line, and another mark 3½ inches (8.9 cm) up from the line. See fig. 2.

To locate the top back rail (I), square a line across the inside face at the point where the curve for the top end starts, or 1¾ inches (4.4 cm) down from the top. Measure in ½ inch (1.3 cm) from the front edge. Make a mark on the line and another 3½ inches (8.9 cm) down from the line.

2. Now position both the bottom and top back rails (H and I) between the back legs (B), aligning them with their respective marks that you made in step 1. Place the bottom rail's lower edge on the lower mark, and the top rail's upper edge on the upper mark. Make sure the front face of each rail is on the marks you made in step 1. Clamp in place.

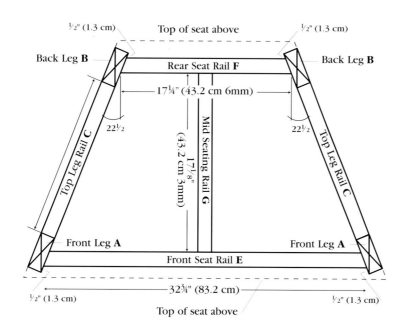

Figure 3

Check that the distance between the bottom edge of the top back rail (I) and the top edge of the bottom back rail (H) is 13 inches (33 cm), and adjust the rails if necessary.

3. Drill two $\frac{1}{16}$-inch (1.6 mm) pilot holes for 12d nails from the outside edge of the back legs (B) into both ends of both back rails (H and I). Secure the back rails (H and I) to the back legs (B), with a 12d nail in each pilot hole. Set the nails, then remove the clamps and check that the joints are tight.

4. You're ready to add the back slats (J). Start by marking the center, lengthwise, on the front face of both the top and bottom back rails (I and H). Then make marks $1\frac{3}{4}$ inch (4.4 cm) on either side of this center mark, and square lines across the top edge of the bottom back rail (H) and the bottom edge of the top back rail (I). This should give you two lines, $3\frac{1}{2}$ inches (8.9 cm) apart, centered on both rails.

5. Place one back slat (J) between the back rails (H and I), centered on the two lines you just made. Adjust the black slat (J) so it's centered on the thickness of the back rails (H and I). Clamp the slat in place. Secure the slat by toe-nailing it into the top and bottom back rails (I and H), using two 4d finish nails at each end. Drive the nails into the edges of the slat, and set their heads with a nail set. Remove the clamp.

6. To locate the two remaining back slats (J), measure $3\frac{1}{2}$ inches (8.9 cm) from one edge of the centered back slat you just installed, and make a mark on the edges of the top and bottom back rails (I and H). Square a line on your

mark. Repeat, working from the opposite edge of the center slat.

7. As you did in step 5, secure the remaining back slats (J) between the back rails (H and I), aligning the inner edges of the slats with the marks you made in step 6. Clamp the slats in place as you nail them, and remember to set the heads.

Finishing the Completed Surround

It's easier to finish all the completed units before you connect them around the tree. Brush the water sealer onto all the surfaces, following the directions on the container.

Assembling the Completed Surround

1. Place all eight units around the tree so that all of the leg assemblies touch. Check that the front edges of the seats are in line, and the surface of the seats are flush to each other. Then clamp the legs together at the front, back, and top.

2. Use two $2\frac{1}{2}$-inch (6.4 cm) screws to connect the units at the following points: the front legs (A); the back legs (B) below the seat; and the back legs (B) above the seat. Conceal the screws above the seat by driving them behind the back rails (H and I).

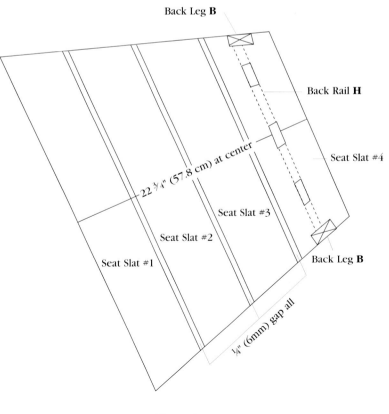

Figure 4

EAT AND RUN CONVERTIBLE
PICNIC TABLE & BENCH

DESIGNER

ALAN MICHAEL HESTER

I*f you enjoy sitting in a favorite outdoor spot for contemplation, and you
love spur-of-the-moment picnics, here's just the project to combine the
two activities. You can transform this comfortable bench into a picnic table and seat—
then back again—in less than a minute.*

TOOLS

Chop saw or radial-arm saw

Jigsaw or band saw

C-clamps

Power drill with $\frac{5}{16}$-inch (8 mm) and $\frac{3}{8}$-inch (9.5 mm) drill bits, and Phillips #2 driver bit

#8 countersink and #8 pilot bit

Socket wrench with $\frac{7}{16}$-inch (1.1 cm) and $\frac{1}{2}$-inch (1.3 cm) sockets, or adjustable wrench

Tape measure

Small square

MATERIALS

Western red cedar

17 linear feet	2 x 4 x 8 stock
30 linear feet	2 x 6 x 8 stock
3 linear feet	2 x 8 x 8 stock

HARDWARE AND SUPPLIES

24 deck screws, #8 x 2½ inches (15.2 x 6.4 cm)

8 carriage bolts, $\frac{5}{16}$ x 3½ inches (8 mm x 8.9 cm) with nuts and washers

2 hex bolts, $\frac{5}{16}$ x 3½ inches (8 mm x 8.9 cm) with nuts and washers

2 eye bolts, $\frac{3}{8}$ x 4 inches (9.5 mm x 10.2 cm)

CUTTING LIST

Code	Description	Qty.	Material	Dimensions
A	Front legs	2	2 x 4 x 8	1½ x 3½ x 17" (3.8 x 8.9 x 43.2 cm) from long point to short point of 10° miter
B	Back legs	2	2 x 4 x 8	1½ x 3½ x 29" (3.8 x 8.9 x 73.7 cm) from long point to short point of 10° miter
C	Crosspieces	2	2 x 4 x 8	1½ x 3½ x 25" (3.8 x 8.9 x 63.5 cm) from long point to short point of 10° miter
D	Back support	1	2 x 4 x 8	1½ x 3½ x 53" (3.8 x 8.9 x 134.6 cm)
E	Seat slats	2	2 x 6 x 8	1½ x 5½ x 6 feet (3.8 x 14 cm x 1.8 m)
F	Top support	2	2 x 8 x 8	1½ x 7¼ x 16" (3.8 x 18.4 x 40.6 cm)
G	Tabletop/back slats	3	2 x 6 x 8	1½ x 5½ x 6 feet (3.8 x 14 cm x 1.8 m)
H	Stop blocks	2	2 x 4 scrap	1½ x 3½ x 3" (3.8 x 8.9 x 7.6 cm) from long point of 10° miter

Making the Base Assembly

1. Dimension the pieces as specified on the cutting list, using the chop saw or the radial-arm saw. Cut complementary 10° miters on both ends of the front and back legs (A and B) and on both ends of the crosspieces (C). The miters give the front and back legs a slight angle for stability and also allow the seat and tabletop to lie flat when you assemble the project.

2. Notch the back legs (B) to receive the back support (D), as shown in fig. 1. Lay out the 3½ x 1½-inch (8.9 x 3.8 cm) notch, 5 inches (12.7 cm) from the short point of the miter at the top of each back leg (B). Use a square to mark the notch, then cut to your layout lines with a jigsaw or on the band saw.

3. Before assembling the base, drill the back legs (B) for the bolts that will connect them to the top supports (F). Locate the hole in each back leg as shown in fig. 1, centering the hole widthwise and 3¾ inches (9.5 cm) from the top of the leg. Drill a 5⁄16-inch (8 mm) hole though each leg.

4. Now you'll assemble the legs to the crosspieces (C). Because you're working with mitered pieces, be careful when assembling the legs. The right and left leg assemblies don't "match." They're mirror images of each other.

For the first assembly, lay a back leg (B) and front leg (A) in front of you. Lay the front leg on top of the back leg, with their bottom ends flush, and mark a line onto the back leg by tracing the miter at the top of the front leg. Then

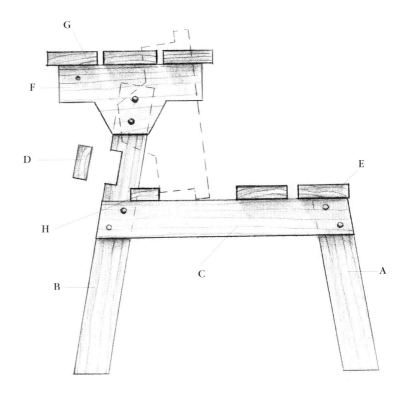

Figure 1

lay a crosspiece (C) on top of the legs, with its top edge flush to the top of the front leg and even with the line you marked on the back leg. The 10° miter at the rear of the crosspiece should align with the rear edge of the back leg, while the short point of the miter at the front of the crosspiece is flush with the outer edge of the front leg. Clamp the assembly.

5. Mark the crosspiece for the carriage bolt holes. With the assembly still clamped, drill a pair of 5⁄16-inch (8 mm) holes at each joint, drilling through the crosspiece and leg. Insert a carriage bolt into each hole, and tight-

en the nut on the inside of the leg with a wrench.

6. Repeat steps 4 and 5 to construct the second leg assembly, making sure you have the mitered pieces in the correct relationship to each other.

7. Now join the two leg assemblies to the back support (D). Fit the back support into the notches in the two leg assemblies, ensuring that the ends of the support are flush with the outer edges of the assemblies. Countersink and drill pilot holes for two #8 x 2½ inch (15.2 x 6.4 cm) screws through each end of the back piece (D) and into the leg assembly, centering the holes on the thickness of the legs. Use the drill and the Phillips driver bit to sink the screws flush with the face of the support.

Building the Seat and Top Supports

1. You're ready to attach the two seat slats (E) to the base assembly. Position the outer edge of the front seat slat (E) on top of the crosspieces and flush with the long point of the miter on the front legs (A). Position the second seat slat (E) next to the first slat, keeping a 1-inch (2.5 cm) gap between the two slats. Make sure the slats are centered lengthwise on the base assembly, with an 8-inch (20.3 cm) overhang on the ends. Drill and countersink as before, driving two screws per joint through the slats and into the crosspieces below.

2. Now you'll make the top supports (F). Lay out the cut lines on each support blank. On each end of the blank, square a line $3\frac{1}{2}$ inches (8.9 cm) below the top edge, and make a mark 4 inches (10.2 cm) in on the line. Then find the center lengthwise of the blank, and mark 2 inches (5.1 cm) on either side of center at the blank's bottom edge. Connect these points to the 4-inch (10.2 cm) marks above using a ruler. Once you've laid out the blanks, use a jigsaw or the band saw to cut the supports to final shape.

3. Drill a $\frac{5}{16}$-inch (8 mm) hole through each top support (F). Center the hole lengthwise on the support, and 2 inches (5.1 cm) up from the bottom edge.

Attaching the Tabletop/Back

1. Now you'll create the top assembly. Attach the three tabletop/back slats (G) to the top supports (F) as shown in fig. 1. Working with the slats upside down on the bench, position the two outer slats so they overhang the supports by 1 inch (2.5 cm) and leave $\frac{3}{4}$-inch (1.9 cm) gaps between individual boards. Check that the overhang on both ends of the slats is 8 inches (20.3 cm) so that the tabletop slats (G) will line up with the seat pieces (E). Clamp the slats to the supports. Then flip the assembly right-side up and countersink and drill pilot holes for #8 x $2\frac{1}{2}$-inch (15.2 x 6.4 cm) screws as you did on the seat slats. Secure the tabletop slats to the top supports using two screws per joint.

2. Slip the top assembly over the base assembly. Match up the holes in the back legs with the holes you drilled in the top supports, and insert a $\frac{5}{16}$-inch (8 mm) hex bolt and washer through each hole. Tighten the nuts on the bolts with a wrench, but don't overtighten. You'll want a little "play" so the bolts can pivot when you raise the tabletop or lower it into its bench seating position.

3. Pivot the tabletop into its horizontal position, and clamp the top supports to the back legs to steady the tabletop. If necessary, use a level to check the top for level. Then drill a $\frac{3}{8}$-inch (9.5 mm) hole through each top support and leg

assembly. You can judge the hole location by eye, drilling it approximately 2 inches (5.1 cm) above the pivot bolt. Insert the $\frac{3}{8}$ x 4-inch (9.5 mm x 10.2 cm) eye bolts through the holes to hold the table firm.

4. Remove the eye bolts and pivot the tabletop down to its alternate position as the bench back. To register the back at a comfortable angle for sitting, add the stop blocks (H) on the crosspieces behind the back. Holding the back in position, clamp the stop blocks so they butt against the back, then pivot the back up and secure it with the eye bolts so it's out of the way. Now screw each block, using two screws per block, to its corresponding crosspiece, countersinking and drilling pilot holes at a slight angle through the block.

5. Finally, you'll need to lock the bench back. First, pivot the tabletop into the bench back position. Working from the inside of each back leg, use a $\frac{3}{8}$-inch (9.5 mm) bit to drill through the back of each existing hole in the legs and through the top support to create a new, matching hole in the top support. When you have the tabletop set up in its alternate bench back position, put the eyebolts through the legs and top supports to secure the back. This also gives you a handy place to keep the bolt when it's not in use!

Extra-Comfy Loveseat

DESIGNER
George Harrison

W*hen you sit in your new loveseat, you'll understand why we think this may be one of the most comfortable garden seats ever crafted. Its lines are inspired by classic Adirondack design, but the difference in comfort is remarkable! The secret is in the templates you'll make and use to cut the contoured pieces of your loveseat.*

MATERIALS

48 linear feet of 1-inch-thick x 5½-inch-wide (2.5 x 14 cm) cypress or pressure-treated lumber

TOOLS

Band saw or jigsaw

Power drill with #8 pilot drill bit, #8 countersink, and ⅛-inch (3 mm) drill bit

Table saw or circular saw with rip guide

Router with ¼-inch (6 mm) roundover bit

C-clamps

Rasp

Measuring tape

Small square

Bevel gauge

Awl

Scrap wood blocks

150-grit sandpaper

HARDWARE AND SUPPLIES

½ sheet (4 x 4 feet) of thin scrap plywood, or stiff cardboard

1 pound #8 x 2-inch (5.1 cm) deck screws

water sealer or paint (optional)

paintbrush (optional)

CUTTING LIST

Code	Description	Qty	Material and Dimensions
A	Seat supports	3	1 x 5½ x 37" (2.5 x 14 x 94 cm), shape as per template
B	Arms	2	1 x 5½ x 31"(2.5 x 14 x 78.7 cm),shape as per template
C	Seat slats	9	1 x 5½ (2.5 x14 cm), 1½ x 42" (3.8 x 106.7 cm)
D	Back slats	4	1 x 5½ x 30" (2.5 x 14 x 76.2 cm), shape as per template
E	Back slats	4	1 x 5½ x 31½" (2.5 x 14 x 80 cm), shape as per template
F	Back slats	4	1 x 5½ x 31½" (2.5 x 14 x 80 cm), shape as per template
G	Arm brackets	2	1 x 5½ x 7⅛" (2.5 x 14 x 18.1 cm), shape as per template
H	Upper back support	1	1 x 5½ x 41½" (2.5 x 14 x 105.4 cm), shape as per template
I	Lower back support	1	1 x 5½ x 42" (2.5 x 14 x 106.7 cm), shape as per template
J	Front legs	2	1 x 5½ x 20⅝" (2.5 x 14 x 52.4 cm), shape as per template
K	Back legs	2	1 x 5½ x 26" (2.5 x 14 x 66 cm), shape as per template

Cutting Out the Chair Parts

1. All of the chair pieces are made using templates, except for the seat slats (C), which you can cut to size on the table saw or with a circular saw. The angles and subtle curves are the key to the loveseat's comfort. If you take your time making the templates, they'll faithfully duplicate the contoured shapes of the chair parts. Enlarge the templates shown on pages 168 and 169 on grid paper, and trace the shapes onto stiff cardboard or thin plywood. Make sure to mark the pilot holes where indicated.

Cut the templates by carefully sawing to your lines with a jigsaw or on the band saw, then fair and smooth the curves with a rasp and 150-grit sandpaper. Drill ⅛-inch (3 mm) holes through the templates at each pilot hole location.

2. Once you've made the templates, lay them on your stock and trace around them. Use an awl to transfer the pilot hole locations onto the stock. Cut out each piece with the jigsaw or on the band saw, cutting up to your traced lines.

3. Countersink and drill all the pilot holes through the chair pieces, except for the back slats (D, E, and F). On these slats, countersink and drill pilot holes only through the lower holes; you'll drill the upper holes later. Be sure to countersink and drill three pilot holes in each seat slat (C), one centered on the slat's length and two holes ½ inch (1.3 cm) in from each end.
4. To ease the sharp edges of the chair,

use the router with the ¼-inch (6 mm) roundover bit. Rout all the edges, or arris, except for those areas where joints will meet. Leave these areas sharp and crisp.

Assembling the Chair Frame

A note about the joinery before you begin assembly: All the joints in this chair are screwed together. You can install the screws much more easily and prevent splitting by boring ⅛-inch (3 mm) pilot holes for the screws in the stock. Once you've aligned the two parts that form a joint, use the ⅛-inch bit to drill through your previously countersunk pilot holes in the first part and into the second, mating piece.

1. On each seat support (A), make a mark 5¾ inches in from the front at the bottom face of the leg. Make another mark at the back of the leg, 2 inches (5.1 cm) in from the back, as shown. You'll use these marks to align the

front and back legs (J and K).

2. Using the straight front edge of your workbench or a straight board as a gauge, position one front leg (J) over one seat support (A), aligning the bottom of the leg and the flat area on the seat support with the straight edge. Position the front leg with the mark you made on the seat support in step 1. Set a bevel gauge to 60°, and use the gauge to position the leg at the correct angle relative to the seat support. Clamp in place. Screw the front leg to the seat support with two #8 x 2-inch (5.1 cm) deck screws. Repeat the process with the second front leg and another seat support, this time arranging the pieces as a mirror image of the first assembly. These assemblies will be used on the right and left sides of the loveseat.

3. Join the right and left sides with the lower back support (I), screwing the support into the notches at the tops of

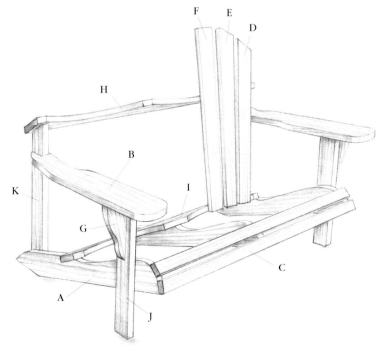

Figure 1

the seat supports (A).

4. Add the remaining seat support (A) by slipping it under the lower back support, then screwing through the back support and into the seat support. If the middle seat support needs stabilizing, add one seat slat (C) at the front of the chair frame, locating it on top of the three seat supports and flush with their bottom front ends.

5. With the chair assembly on a flat surface, such as a benchtop or the floor, use a square to position the back legs (K) square to each seat support (A). Align the legs to the marks you made in step 1. Clamp the legs, then screw them to the supports.

Attaching the Arms

1. Before you attach the arms (B), secure the arm brackets (G) to the front legs (J) to support them. Clamp the brackets flush with the tops of the legs, then screw through the legs and into the brackets, using two screws per bracket.

2. Position the arms (B) on top of the brackets (G), making sure the notch in the back of each arm fits snugly against the back leg (K). Trim the notch if necessary. At the front of the chair, screw each arm (B) into the top of its corresponding arm bracket (G) and front leg (J). Then level each arm by measuring the distance of the arm to the floor at the front of the chair, and use that measurement to adjust the back of the arm relative to the back leg (K). Once the arms are level, screw through the back legs and into the arms to secure them.

Adding the Backs and Seat

1. Position the upper back support (H) on top of the two back legs (K), making sure the support is flush on its inner edge with the inner edges of the legs. Secure the support by screwing through it and into the tops of the legs, using two screws per joint.

2. The back slats (D, E, and F) are arranged in three groups of descending heights, as shown in fig. 1. Start with the two outermost slats for each back, positioning the bottoms of the slats

with the bottom face of the lower back support (I). Align the outer slats with the outer edges of the curves in the upper and lower back supports (H and I). Once you've positioned the slats, mark and drill them for the upper countersink and pilot holes, making sure the holes are centered over the thickness of the upper back support (H). Screw the slats to the supports, using one screw per joint. Now arrange the remaining slats in the correct order, spacing them equally from each other by eye. Mark and drill the countersinks and pilot holes as before, then screw the back slats to the upper and lower supports.

3. If you've already attached one seat slat (C) to the chair, you're left with eight more to install. Start by attaching one seat slat (C) at the rear, positioning it against the back slats and screwing it to all three seat supports. Then arrange the remaining seven seat slats so there's equal spacing or gaps between all nine slats. You can arrange the slats by eye, or use scrap wood blocks of the correct thickness to help achieve even gaps. Screw the seat slats (C) to the seat supports (A) as before, using three screws per slat.

4. Finish the project by brushing on an application of water sealer if desired, following package directions, or paint the chair if you wish. Once the finish has dried, find a loved one and put the chair to use!

GARDEN PERIMETER BENCH

This spacious bench serves double-duty, giving you plenty of sitting room around the garden while it also serves as an attractive surface for potted plants. It's also very easy to modify the length and proportions of the bench to suit the needs of your garden.

MATERIALS

Weather-resistant woods such as cedar, teak, Honduras mahogany, or pressure-treated pine are recommended for this project.

24 linear feet (7.2 linear meters)	4 x 4 x 8 stock
88 linear feet (26.4 linear meters)	2 x 4 x 8 stock
12 linear feet (3.6 linear meters)	2 x 4 x 12 stock

HARDWARE AND SUPPLIES

Bag of sand and gravel concrete mix (optional)

Water (optional)

Mixing bucket (optional)

32 #10 x 3-inch (25 x 7.5 cm) wood screws

88 #8 x 2½-inch (20 x 6.25 cm) wood screws

Clear water sealer with UV protectors and mildew inhibitor

Paintbrush

TOOLS

Handsaw or circular saw

Tape measure

Small square

C-clamps

Bar-style clamps, 4 feet (120 cm) long

Scrap wood blocks

2-foot (60 cm) or longer level

Shovel or post hole digger

Power drill with #8 and #10 countersink and pilot bits

Screwdriver

CUTTING LIST

The parts listed make up one 8-foot-long (240 cm) section of bench. You can make it longer or shorter as desired, as long as you place the bench supports a maximum of 2 feet (60 cm) apart. You can also make the bench wider or narrower by adjusting the length of the rails and the number of slats. Adjust the width in 3⅝-inch (9 cm) increments, the width of a slat plus a slight gap. You also have the option of making the bench in sections, and assembling it by screwing or bolting two adjacent frames together.

Code	Description	Qty.	Material and Dimensions
A	Post	8	4 x 4 x 32" (10 x 10 x 80 cm)
B	Rail	4	2 x 4 x 36" (5 x 10 x 90 cm)
C	Slat	11	2 x 4 x 8' (60 x 120 x 240 cm)

INSTRUCTIONS

Making the Frames

1. Cut the eight posts (A) and the four rails (B) to length.

2. On one face of all four rails (B), measure 3½ inches (8.75 cm) in from each end, and square a line across the face of the rail.

3. Lay two posts (A) on your bench about 29 inches (72.5 cm) apart. Lay one rail (B) across the posts so that the marks you made in step 2 are even with the outside edges of the posts, and the edge of the rail is flush to the ends of the posts. Clamp in place to prevent any movement.

4. Drill four countersunk pilot holes for #10 x 3 inch (25 x 7.5 cm) screws from the rail (B) into each post (A) at their intersections. Then attach the rail to each post with four screws.

5. Repeat steps 3 and 4 to assemble three more frames with the remaining posts (A) and rails (B).

Installing the Frames and Adding the Seat

1. At your chosen garden location, use the shovel or post hole digger to dig two holes approximately 6 inches (15 cm) in diameter, 16 inches (40 cm) deep, and 29 inches (72.5 cm) apart. The holes will accommodate one frame assembly.

2. Place the frame in the holes. The posts (A) should be sunk 16 inches (40 cm) in the ground. Use the level to make sure the rail (B) is level and the posts are plumb, i.e., vertical.

3. Start filling in the dirt around the posts (A), 3 or 4 inches (7.5 or 10 cm) at a time, packing it in around the posts. If the dirt doesn't compact well or is sandy, make a concrete mix according to package directions using the sand, concrete, and water. Mix the ingredients in the bucket, then fill in around the posts to ground level with the mixture and allow the concrete to set.

4. Once you have one of the frames secured in the ground, dig holes for the remaining frames 2 feet (60 cm) apart. Set the other three frames level with the first. You can easily check for level by laying one of your straightest 2 x 4 (5 x 10 cm) slats across all four frames and placing the level on top. Backfill the holes around the frames with dirt, or fill with the concrete mix and allow the concrete to set.

5. Place one of the slats (C) on top of the frames so that it overhangs the ends of the rails (B) by ½ inch (1.25 cm). Drill two countersunk pilot holes for #8 x 2½-inch (6.25 cm) screws through the face of the slat (C) into each rail (B). Secure the slat to each rail using two screws per rail.

6. Place another slat (C) at the opposite end of the frame, this time aligning the edge of the slat flush wtih the ends of the rails (B). Secure the slat as you did the first slat in step 5.

7. Place eight of the slats (C) between the two you've just attached to the frame, spacing them equally and attaching them to the rails (B) as before. If necessary, use scrap spacer blocks of the correct thickness between the slats to help create even gaps.

8. Take the last slat (C) and position its face against the edge of the back slat so that it's vertical and forms a lip. Clamp the slat to the bench with bar clamps. Drill a series of countersunk pilot holes for #8 x 2½-inch (6.25 cm) screws, drilling through the slat and into the edge of the back slat, spacing the holes roughly 12 inches (30 cm) apart. Secure the vertical slat with screws.

9. Brush the water sealer over every surface of the bench and allow to dry.

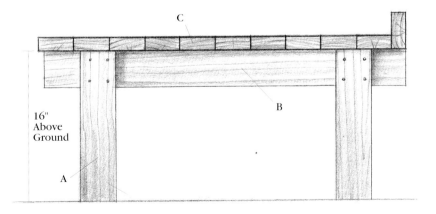

Figure 1

ROMANTIC SHELTERED GARDEN BENCH

I*nvite a friend over for a* kaffeklatsch *on this fabulous bench, and you can almost imagine yourself in a charming spot in Old Europe. Scalloped trim on the eaves and ready-made lattice on the sides add pretty detail. When you purchase pillows for the seat, select bright mix-and-match prints to add to the casual, comfortable mood. You'll be happiest making this project if you're an experienced woodworker, or if you have a knowledgeable friend to help you.*

MATERIALS

62 linear feet	2 x 4 cedar
20 linear feet	1 x 2 cedar
70 linear feet	1 x 6 tongue-and-groove spruce
30 linear feet	1 x 6 cedar
4 linear feet	1 x 12 cedar

4 feet x 4 feet sheet of ½-inch-thick exterior-grade plywood

4 feet x 4 feet sheet of ¼-inch lattice screen

TOOLS

Tape measure

Small square

Handsaw

Table saw (optional)

Router with edge guide and ½-inch (1.3 cm) straight bit and ¼-inch (6 mm) chamfering bit (optional)

Circular saw with a rip guide

Bar-style clamps in assorted lengths from 30 to 36 inches (76.2 to 91.4 cm)

Scrap wood blocks

⅜-inch (9.5 mm) power drill with #8 pilot drill bit and #8 countersink

Hammer

Jigsaw

Palm or random-orbit sander

HARDWARE AND SUPPLIES

40 #8 x 3-inch wood screws

½ lb. 4d finish nails

20 #8 x 1½-inch wood screws

40 #8 x 2½-inch wood screws

4 8d finish nails

150 grit sandpaper

Rags

Exterior-grade stain, or oil-based or latex enamel paint

Paintbrush

CUTTING LIST

Code	Description	Qty.	Material and Dimensions
A	Post	4	2 x 4 x 56 ½" (143.5 cm)
B	Top rail	2	2 x 4 x 17" (43.2 cm)
C	Mid rail	2	2 x 4 x 17" (43.2 cm)
D	Foot	2	2 x 4 x 23½" (59.7 cm)
E	Foot pad	4	½-inch plywood, 3½ x 3½" (8.9 x 8.9 cm)
F	Side panel cleat	4	¾ x ¾ x 17" (43.2 cm)
G	Side boards	8	tongue-and-groove, 1 x 6 x 13¾" (34.9 cm)
H	Lattice cleat	4	¾ x ¾ x 36¼" (1.9 x 1.9 x 92 cm)
I	Lattice	2	17 x 36¼" (43.2 x 92 cm)
J	Seat rail	2	2 x 4 x 43" (109.2 cm)
K	Seat support	3	2 x 4 x 15¼" (38.7 cm)
L	Seat boards	5	1 x 6 x 43" (109.2 cm)
M	Lower back rail	1	2 x 4 x 43" (109.2 cm)
N	Mid back rail	1	1 x 12 x 43" (109.2 cm)
O	Back boards	10	tongue-and-groove, 1 x 6 x various
P	Roof rail	4	2 x 4 x 30" (76.2 cm)
Q	Roof support	4	2 x 4 x 13" (33 cm)
R	Roof	2	½-inch plywood, 20¾ x 30" (52.7 x 76.2 cm)
S	Fascia	4	1 x 6 x 32" (81.3 cm)
T	Finial*	1	about 12" (30.5 cm) long; style as desired

*Readymade finials are available in varied designs at home improvement stores.

INSTRUCTIONS

Making the Side Frames

1. Use the tape measure and a pencil to measure and mark all four posts (A), then cut them to length with the handsaw or table saw. If desired, use the router with the chamfering bit to rout decorative, ¼-inch-wide (6 mm) stopped chamfers on the front faces of the two front posts, as shown in the photograph.

2. Use the router equipped with the edge guide and the ½-inch (1.3 cm) straight bit, or the table saw, to make a ¾-inch-deep (1.9 cm) by 2-inch-wide (5.1 cm) rabbet on the back face of each of the two posts (A) as shown in fig. 1. If you use the router, make several shallow cuts to reach the full depth.

3. Use the circular saw or handsaw to cut the two top rails (B) and two mid rails (C) to length.

4. On the inside face of the four posts (A), measure 17¼ inches (43.8 cm) in from one end, and use the square and pencil to square a line across the boards.

5. Lay two of the posts (A) on the work surface, with one edge facing up and the inside faces pointing toward each other. Place one top rail (B) between the posts, aligned with their top ends. Place one mid rail (C) between the posts with the top face on the line you made in step 4. All edges should be flush. Clamp the assembly to keep the pieces from moving, and join them by driving screws through the posts and into the rails. Use the #8 pilot bit and countersink to predrill two pilot holes at each joint, then drive two 3-inch

(7.6 cm) wood screws into each joint.

6. Place one foot (D) against the bottom ends of the two posts (see fig. 2). Predrill and countersink pilot holes, then attach the foot to the posts with two 3-inch (7.6 cm) wood screws at each joint.

7. Nail the two plywood foot pads (E) to the foot (D) as indicated in fig. 2, using four 4d finish nails per pad.

8. Nail one side panel cleat (F) to the top face of the foot (D) and the bottom face of the mid rail (C) with four 4d finish nails evenly spaced along its length. The cleats should be flush to the inside edges of the foot and mid rail.

9. Crosscut the four tongue-and-groove side boards (G) to fit the space between the mid rail (C) and the foot (D). Assemble the boards into their tongues and grooves, then compare the width of the assembly with the space between the two posts (A). Rip the outer edges of the two outside boards with the circular saw or the table saw so the assembly fits between the posts. Once the panel fits, nail it to the side panel cleats (F) using two 4d finish nails on each board end.

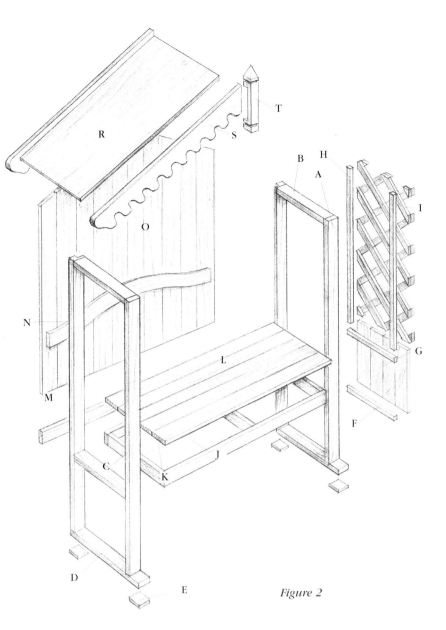

Figure 2

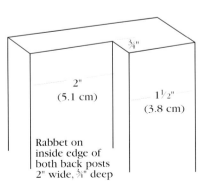

Figure 1

10. Nail one lattice cleat (H) to the inside face of each post (A), using six 4d finish nails evenly spaced along its length. The cleats should be flush to the inside edges of the posts.

11. Nail one lattice panel (I) to the lattice cleats (H). Use 4d finish nails, driving a nail through the end of each lattice strip.

12. Now you'll make the second side frame. Repeat steps 5 through 11 and assemble the remaining posts (A), rails

(B and C), foot and foot pads (D and E), side boards (G), and lattice (I).

Adding the Seat and Back Rail

1. Locate the center, lengthwise, on each of the two seat rails (J), and mark it on one face of each rail. This will be the inside face.

2. Lay the two seat rails (J) on the work surface with one edge facing up and the inside faces pointing toward each other. Place the three seat supports (K) between the rails, one support at each end of the rails and one support centered on the mark you just made. Clamp the pieces together, and assemble the frame using two 3-inch (7.6 cm) wood screws at each joint. Predrill and countersink all holes.

3. Now you'll attach the seat boards (L) to the assembled seat frame. You'll need to rip the back seat board to a width that will fit. Start with the front seat board, which should overhang the front seat rail (J) by 1 inch (2.1 cm). Predrill and countersink all holes, then drive two 1½-inch (3.8 cm) screws into each seat support (K) per board, using a total of six screws per board.

4. On the inside edge of the two assembled side frames, measure up 18 inches (45.7 cm) from the bottom face of the foot (D), and make a mark on each post (A).

5. Position the two side frames on the work surface or floor with their back posts facing down and their inside faces toward each other. Place the seat assembly between the side frames with the top of the seat boards on the mark you made in step 4. Use scrap spacer blocks under the seat assembly so the back seat rail (J) is flush with the rabbet in the back posts (A). Clamp the seat assembly to the side frames, and join the assemblies with screws. Drive two 2½-inch (6.4 cm) screws through the outside seat supports (K) and into the back posts (A), and two more screws through the outside seat supports into the front posts. Predrill and countersink all holes.

6. Place the lower back rail (M) between the side frames with its bottom

face flush with the bottom face of both feet (D). Its back edge should be flush with the face of the rabbet in the back posts (A). Clamp in place, and secure the lower back rail (M) to the feet (D) with two 2½-inch (6.4 cm) wood screws at each end. Predrill and countersink all holes, driving the screws at an angle from the edges of the rail into the edges of the feet.

Making and Attaching the Roof

1. Miter one end on each of four roof rails (P) to 22.75°, using the circular saw or the table saw, then cut the rails to length. Using the same miter angle, rip a miter along the long edge of two roof supports (Q).

2. With two roof rails (P) face up on the work surface, place two of the roof supports (Q) between them, one at each end, aligning one of the mitered supports with the mitered ends of the rails (see fig. 3). Clamp the frame, then secure the parts using two 2½-inch (6.4 cm) wood screws per joint. Insert the screws at an angle from each edge of the roof support (Q) into the edge of the roof rail (P).

3. With the circular saw or the table saw, miter one edge of each roof (R) to 22.75°. Position one roof (R) over the assembled roof frame, with its miter aligned with the mitered frame. The roof should extend past the outside edge of one roof rail by ¾ inch (1.9 cm), while it is flush with the outside edge of the opposing roof rail. Attach the roof with the 4d finish nails spaced 4 inches (10.2 cm) on center around the edges of the roof.

4. To create the other roof panel, repeat steps 2 and 3.

5. Position the two roof panels on the two side frames so that the mitered roof supports meet to form the peak. The ends of each panel should extend beyond the side panels by about 5 inches (12.5 cm) and the ¾-inch (1.9 cm) plywood roof overhang should be flush with the outside faces of the back posts. Clamp the roof panels in place. Secure the roof panels to each other at the peak using four 2½-inch (6.4 cm) wood screws driven in at an angle from one roof support (Q) into the opposing roof support. Then attach the ends of each roof panel to the side panels by driving two 2½-inch (6.4 cm) screws through the roof rails (P) and into each post (A). Predrill and countersink all holes.

Attaching the Back

1. Starting in the center between the two back posts (A), insert the tongue-and-groove back boards (O) between the roof (R) and the bottom face of the lower back rail (M). Miter the top end of each back board to 22.75°, then crosscut it to length as required. Work from the center toward both posts. Attach the back boards to the lower back rail (M) and the back roof rail (P) using two 4d finish nails at each end per board. You'll need to rip the two outer boards to a width that fits.

2. Refer to figure 4 and use grid paper to enlarge the curved mid back rail (N) to the dimensions shown. Place the template over the 1 x 12 rail stock and trace the outline. Use the jigsaw to cut the mid back rail to shape, and smooth any irregularities with sandpaper or a pad sander.

3. Attach the mid back rail (N) to the back boards (O) using two 4d finish nails in each back board. Before nailing, position the two lower, outer ends of the mid back rail so they're 8 inches (20.3 cm) above the top of the seat.

Adding the Fascia and Finial

1. Miter one end on each of the four 1 x 6 fascia blanks to 22.75° with the circular saw. Then use a photocopier to enlarge the fascia template to the dimensions shown in fig. 5. Transfer the template design to the blanks. Use the jigsaw to cut out the decorative fascia (S). Nail it to the roof rails (P) at the front and back using 4d finish nails spaced about 4 inches (10.2 cm) apart along the length of the fascia.

2. Now you'll add the finial (T) to the front fascia boards. Use the router and the ½-inch (1.3 cm) straight bit or the table saw to cut a dado on the back of the finial to fit it over the fascia, as shown in fig. 2. Secure the finial to the peak by driving two 8d finish nails through the finial and into the fascia and the front roof rails (P).

3. Use the sandpaper and the pad sander to smooth all rough edges, and wipe away dust with the dampened rag. Let dry, then stain or paint the entire assembly. Let dry, then place the cushions on the bench.

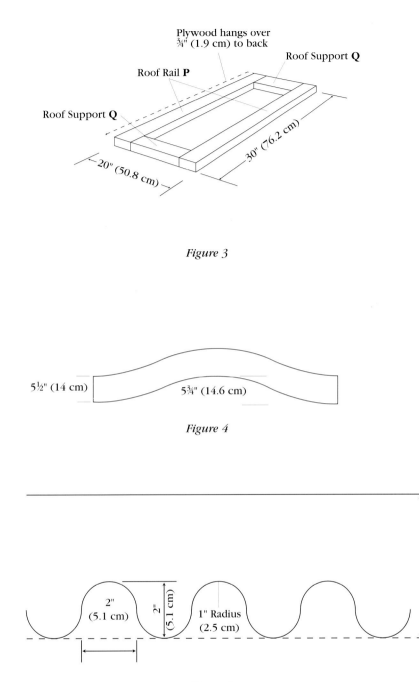

Plywood hangs over ¾" (1.9 cm) to back

Roof Support **Q**

Roof Rail **P**

Roof Support **Q**

20" (50.8 cm)

30" (76.2 cm)

Figure 3

5½" (14 cm)

5¾" (14.6 cm)

Figure 4

2" (5.1 cm)

2" (5.1 cm)

1" Radius (2.5 cm)

Figure 5

5½"

Easy Living Trestle Swing

Swings suspended from freestanding trestles were very popular with the Victorian gentry, and they're popular again today because of their versatility. This project doesn't require a porch or tree for hanging, only a flat area to stand on. The gently curved seat and back are very comfortable, and its size makes it a cozy swing for two.

MATERIALS

88 linear feet	1 x 2 cedar
4 linear feet	1 x 4 cedar
6 linear feet	2 x 4 cedar
6 linear feet	2 X 6 cedar
12 linear feet	2 X 8 cedar
42 linear feet	6 x 6 cedar

**For Cutting List, see page 114.

TOOLS

Tape measure

Scissors

Small compass

Rafter angle square (speed square)

Handsaw

Jigsaw

Circular saw with rip guide

Table saw (optional)

Power drill with #8 pilot drill bit and #8 countersink

¼-inch (6 mm) drill bit; ¾-inch (1.9 mm) and ⅞-inch (2.2 cm) spade bits

C-clamps

Bar-style clamps in assorted lengths from 30 to 36 inches (76.2 to 91.44 cm)

Scrap wood blocks

Palm or random-orbit sander

HARDWARE AND SUPPLIES

Thin plywood or stiff cardboard to make templates

100 #8 x 1½-inch (3.8 cm) wood screws

12 #8 x 2½-inch (6.4 cm) wood screws

28 #8 x 3-inch (7.6 cm) wood screws

2 screw eyes, ⅜ x 1½-inch (9.5 mm x 3.8 cm)

2 screws eyes, ⅜ x 2½-inch (9.5 cm x 6.4 cm)

2 screw eyes, ½ x 3-inch (1.3 x 7.6 cm)

4 lag bolts, ½ x 5-inch (1.3 x 12.7 cm)

8 lag bolts, ½ x 8-inch (1.3 x 20.3 cm)

4 S-hooks, 1½ inches (3.8 cm)

2 lengths of ⅛-inch (3 mm) chain, each 6 feet (1.8 m) long

150-grit sandpaper

Rags

Exterior wood stain

Paintbrush

A helpful friend

INSTRUCTIONS

Building the Seat

1. Use the grid pattern shown in fig. 1 to enlarge full-size templates for the curved back supports (A) and seat supports (B). Draw the templates on stiff cardboard or thin plywood, and cut them out with scissors or with a jigsaw depending on the material. Use the templates to trace the three back supports (A) and the three seat supports (B) onto your stock. Then saw out the curved pieces with a jigsaw.

2. Cut the half-lap joints on the back supports (A) and seat supports (B), as shown in fig. 2. Each piece has a tongue that's half the thickness of the wood. Lay out the joints and cut them with a handsaw or on the table saw. Test-fit the pieces, adjusting the depth of cut if necessary.

3. Fit one half-lap joint together, making sure the shoulders are tight, then clamp the back and seat supports to the work surface. Countersink and drill five pilot holes for #8 x 1½-inch (3.8 cm) screws through the back support (A) and into the seat support (B), spacing the holes evenly across the lap joint. Secure the joint with five screws, and set the seat assembly aside.

4. Assemble two more seat assemblies from the two remaining back supports (A) and seat supports (B), following step 3.

5. Cut the four seat rails (C) to length.

6. Now secure the seat rails (C) to the seat assemblies. Working with the first assembly, align two seat rails (C) with the bottom edge of the seat support (B), one at the rear and one at the front as

CUTTING LIST

Code	Description	Qty.	Material	Dimensions
A	Back supports	3	2 x 8	$1\frac{1}{2}$ x $7\frac{1}{4}$ x 40" (3.8 x 18.4 cm x 101.6 cm) shape as per template
B	Seat supports	3	2 x 6	$1\frac{1}{2}$ x $5\frac{1}{2}$ x 24" (3.8 x 14 x 61 cm) shape as per template
C	Seat rails	4	2 x 4	$1\frac{1}{2}$ x $3\frac{1}{2}$ x $21\frac{3}{4}$" (3.8 x 8.9 x 55.2 cm)
D	Top slat	1	1 x 4	$\frac{3}{4}$ x $3\frac{1}{2}$ x 50" (1.9 x 8.9 x 127 cm)
E	Seat slats	22	1 x 2	$\frac{3}{4}$ x $3\frac{1}{2}$ x 50" (1.9 x 8.9 x 127 cm)
F	Arms	2	2 x 4	$1\frac{1}{2}$ x $3\frac{1}{2}$ x 22" (3.8 x 8.9 x 55.9 cm)
G	Arm supports	9	2 x 4	$1\frac{1}{2}$ x $3\frac{1}{2}$ x $12\frac{1}{2}$" (3.8 x 8.9 x 31.8 cm)
H	Trestle legs	4	6 x 6	$5\frac{1}{2}$ x $5\frac{1}{2}$ x 84" (14 x 14 x 213.4 cm) from long point to long point of miters
I	Side rails	2	6 x 6	$5\frac{1}{2}$ x $5\frac{1}{2}$ x 24" (14 x 14 x 61 cm) from long point to long point of miters
J	Corner braces	2	6 x 6	$5\frac{1}{2}$ x $5\frac{1}{2}$ x 11" (14 x 14 x 27.9 cm) from long point to long point of miters
K	Top beam	1	6 x 6	$5\frac{1}{2}$ x $5\frac{1}{2}$ x 72" (14 x 14 x 182.9 cm)

supports, and countersink and drill two pilot holes for #8 x 3-inch (7.6 cm) screws through the seat support and into the end of each rail. Space the holes approximately $\frac{3}{4}$ inch (1.9 cm) from the top and bottom edges of the rails. Secure the rails to the supports with two screws at each joint.

7. Repeat step 6 to attach the remaining two seat rails to another seat assembly.

You should now have two seat assemblies, with two seat rails attached to each, and one seat assembly with no rails.

8. With your friend's help, stand the two seat assemblies that have rails upright on the work surface, pointing the rails toward each other. Position the remaining seat assembly between

the rails, and lightly clamp all three assemblies together. Adjust the rails on the middle seat assembly as needed, and tighten the clamps. Countersink and drill two pilot holes for 3-inch (7.6 cm) screws through each side of the middle seat assembly and into the ends of each rail. You'll need to toe-nail the holes by drilling at an angle since the rails are directly opposite each other. Secure the rails by driving screws through the seat assembly and into the ends of the rails.

Adding the Seat Slats

1. Cut all the seat slats (E), including the top slat (D), to length. Before you assemble the slats, smooth and round over any sharp edges with 150-grit sandpaper and a pad sander.

2. Place the top slat (D) in line with the tops of the back supports (A) and even with their outside faces, and clamp it in place. Countersink and drill two pilot holes through each end and in the middle of the slat for $1\frac{1}{2}$-inch (3.8 cm) screws, centering the holes over the back supports. Then secure the top slat (D) to the back supports, using a total of six screws.

3. Now you can add the seat slats (E), starting below the top slat (D). To create even gaps between all the slats, position three $\frac{3}{4}$-inch-thick (1.9 cm) scrap spacer blocks between the top slat and the first seat slat, placing a spacer over each seat assembly. Align the seat slat so its ends are even with the back supports (A) and with the top slat (D) above. Clamp the slat in place, or have your friend hold it steady while you countersink and drill one pilot hole for a 1½-inch (3.8 cm) screw through the slat and into each seat support. Screw the seat slat (E) to the back supports, using a total of three screws.

4. Repeat step 3 to attach all of the seat slats (E) to the back and seat supports (A and B) of the swing.

Making and Attaching the Arms

1. Cut out the two arms (F) and the two arm supports (G). Lay out the 1¾-inch (4.4 cm) radius on the ends of the arms with a compass, then cut the curves by sawing to the lines with a jigsaw.

2. Square a line across the bottom face of one arm (F), 2 inches (5.1 cm) back from its curved front edge. Clamp one arm support (G) to the arm so that its face is flush with the inner edge of the arm and one edge of the support is on the line you just marked. Countersink and drill two pilot holes for 3-inch (7.6 cm) screws through the arm and into the arm support, and screw the support to the arm.

3. Repeat step 2 to attach the other arm to its support.

4. Position one arm assembly against one end of the swing. Check that the back of the arm is flush with the back edge of the back support (A), and that the bottom of the arm support (G) is flush with the bottom of the seat support (B). Clamp the assembly in place, and countersink and drill two pilot holes from the inside face of the back support (A) and into the arm (F). Center the holes in the arm, and secure it to the back support with two 2½-inch (6.4 cm) screws. Similarly, attach the

arm support (G) at the front of the assembly by countersinking and drilling four pilot holes from the inside face of the seat support (B) and into the arm support. Secure the support with four 2½-inch (6.4 cm) screws.

5. Repeat step 4 to attach the remaining arm assembly to the opposite side of the swing.

6. With the swing constructed, you can install the hanging hardware. Drill two ¾-inch (1.9 cm) holes through each arm (F) with a spade bit for the hanging chain to pass through. Locate the first hole 3 inches (7.6 cm) in from the back of each arm and centered on its width. Drill the second hole toward the front of the arm, centered widthwise and directly adjacent to the arm support.

7. Install one ⅜ x 1½-inch (9.5 x 3.8 cm) screw eye into each outer back support (A), and one ⅜ x 2½-inch (9.5 x 6.4 cm) screw eye through each arm support (G) and into each outer seat support (B). Drill a ¼-inch (6 mm) pilot hole for each screw, locating the holes 2 inches (5.1 cm) from the bottom of the arm supports and back supports and centered on their width.

Building the Trestle

1. With the swing complete, you're ready to tackle the trestle. Cut out the four trestle legs (H), the two side rails (I), and the two corner braces (J). Using the rafter angle square and circular saw, mark and cut the legs (H) with a 70° miter on the top ends, and a 20° miter on the bottom ends. Make sure the miters oppose each other so that the long points of the miters are on the same face of the beam. Mark

and cut 20° opposing miters on each end of the side rails (I). Clamp the brace stock (J) to a work surface, then mark and cut 20° opposing miters on each end. The top face of each brace should come to a point. Set the corner braces (J) aside for now.

2. Position two trestle legs (H) on the floor with their top miters touching. Then place one side rail (I) between the legs roughly halfway down their length, or until the miters of the rail fit snug between the legs. Check that the rail is level and square with the legs by measuring up from the bottom of each leg. Clamp the miter joint at the top of the legs and clamp the rail between the legs.

3. Drill one ⅜-inch (9.5 mm) pilot hole through each leg (H) and into the ends of the side rail (I), and one hole through one leg at the top miter joint and into the opposite leg. Drill the holes in the legs and rails about 8 inches (20.3 cm) deep. Drill the holes in the miter joints at the top of the legs 5 inches (12.7 cm) deep. When drilling for the side rail, angle the bit to the leg so the holes are parallel to the rail. Center the holes on the width of the leg and rail, and center the holes over the joint at the top of the legs. Join the mitered legs (H) with a 5-inch (12.7 cm) lag bolt, and secure the side rail (I) to the legs with two 8-inch (20.3 cm) lag bolts. Remove the clamps.

4. Repeat step 2 to assemble the remaining two legs (H) and rail (I) into a second A-frame unit.

5. Cut the top beam (K) to length. On both ends of the beam, mark a line across the bottom face 5½ inches (14 cm) in

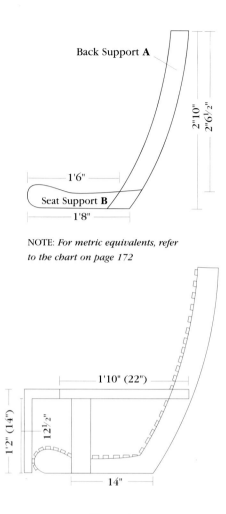

Back Support A

2"10"
2"6½"

1'6"

Seat Support B

1'8"

NOTE: *For metric equivalents, refer to the chart on page 172*

1'10" (22")

1'2" (14")

12½"

14"

Figure 1

from the end, and mark another line across the end itself 2¾ inches (7 cm) from the top face. Cut to your marked lines with a handsaw or circular saw to form a rabbet 2-3/4 inches (7 cm) deep x 5½ inches (14 cm) long at each end of the beam.

6. Going back to the A-frame assemblies, measure about 7 inches (17.8 cm) down from the top of each miter joint, and square a line around the legs. The line should be 5½ inches wide (14 cm), or the width of the top beam (K), on the inside and outside faces of the A-frame. Cut to your layout lines with a circular saw and remove the

waste to create a flat area at the top of the A-frames for the top beam (K).

7. Enlisting your friend's help once again, stand the two A-frames upright at their intended resting spot, and place the top beam (K) across the frames. Make sure the shoulders of the rabbets you cut in the beam are snug to the inside faces of the frames. At each end of the beam, drill a ⅜-inch (9.5 mm) pilot hole through the top of the beam and into the leg assembly, centered on the miter joint. Secure the beam to the top of the trestle with a 5-inch (12.7 cm) lag bolt at each end.

8. Stiffen the trestle to prevent racking by adding the two corner braces (J). Position each brace inside the frame between the top beam (K) and the miter joint at the top of the A-frame, and clamp it in place. Drill a ⅜-inch (9.5 cm) pilot hole through each end of the brace and into the beam and frame, angling the bit as you drill. Drill the holes about 8 inches (20.3 cm) deep, then secure each brace to the beam and frame with two 8-inch (20.3 cm) lag bolts.

9. Now install the hanging hardware on the trestle. On the bottom face of the top beam (K), measure 12 inches (30.5 cm) in from both ends, and drill a ⅜-inch (9.5 mm) pilot hole centered on the beam's width. Install a 3-inch (7.6 cm) screw eye into each hole at each end of the beam.

10. Using two lengths of chain and four S-hooks, hang the swing from the trestle. Use the S-hooks to attach the chain to the screw eyes in both the trestle and the swing. Be sure to pass the chain through the holes in the arms

(F) of the swing before attaching it to the screw eyes. Adjust the length of the chain to provide a comfortable sitting and swinging height. Sixteen to 18 inches (40.6 cm to 45.7 cm) from the seat to the ground is optimum.

11. Finish the trestle swing by sanding all the parts smooth and rounding over any sharp edges. Then wipe off any dust with a dampened rag, and paint the swing with an exterior wood stain in the color of your choice.

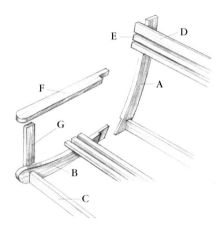

E   D

F   A

G

B

C

Figure 2

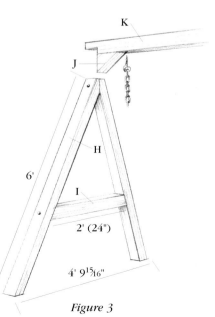

K

J

H

6'

I

2' (24")

4' 9¹⁵⁄₁₆"

Figure 3

Classic English Garden Bench

DESIGNERS
Ray Martin and Lee Rankin

*T*his stately oak bench will provide a classical counterpoint in your garden, while the gentle arc of the back and its slat design evoke a sense of calm. If your woodworking repetoire includes traditional joinery, you'll enjoy making the strong mortise-and-tenon joints used at all points of construction. This is the type of seat from which you can sip a cup of tea, survey your estate, and take the long view of things.

MATERIALS

White oak, which holds up well outdoors, was used to create the bench. Other suitable outdoor woods for the bench are cypress, Honduras mahogany, and teak.

16 linear feet	½ x 2½ " oak
31 linear feet	1 x 2½ " oak
5-1/2 linear feet	1 x 7" oak
3 linear feet	1¾ x 1¾" oak
18 linear feet	1¾ x 2½ " oak
4 linear feet	1¾ x 3½ " oak
6 linear feet	1¾x 5¼" oak
¼ x 5 x 36" plywood	
¼ x 7 x 62" plywood	

HARDWARE AND SUPPLIES

2 small nails or brads

Scrap wood blocks

15 deck screws, #6 x 2 inches (12.95 cm)

15 tapered wood plugs

Pull-chain or nylon cord, 6-foot (1.8 cm) long

150-grit sandpaper

Exterior wood glue

TOOLS

Tape measure

Combination square

Small compass

Ruler or straightedge, 24 feet (61 mm)

Hammer

Level

Bench chisels, ¼ inch (6 mm) and ½ inch (1.3 cm)

Rasp

Bevel gauge

Backsaw

Spokeshave (optional)

Hand plane (optional)

Drill press with mortising attachment, or tablesaw with dado blade or tenoning jig

Power drill with #6 counterbore, #6 countersink, and #6 pilot bit

Circular saw

Jigsaw

Band saw (optional)

C-clamps

Bar-style clamps in assorted lengths from 30 to 72 inches (76.2 to 180 cm)

Palm or random-orbit sander

INSTRUCTIONS

Making the Templates for the Legs and Back Rail

1. You'll use plywood templates to generate the curves on the top back rail (A) and the angles on the back legs (E). Start with the 62-inch-long (157.5 cm) piece of plywood noted in the materials list to make the rail template. Position the long edge of the plywood on the work surface. Use clamps if necessary to hold it upright. Level the plywood from end to end. You can do this by inserting shims under it and checking it with a level or the bubble gauge in the combination square.

2. On each end of the plywood, mark a point 3¾ inches (9.5 cm) down from the top edge, as shown in fig. 1. From these two points, attach a pull-chain or heavy nylon cord using small brads or nails, allowing the chain to sag the full width of the board, or 7 inches (45.21 cm). The shallow curve formed is called a catenary curve. Use a pencil to trace around the outer edge of the curve, being careful not to disturb the chain. Cut to your curved line with a jigsaw or on the band saw, making sure to saw on the waste side of the line.

Code	Description	Qty.	Dimensions
A	Top back rail*	1	1 x 7 x 62" (2.5 x 17.8 x 157.5 cm)
B	Bottom back rail*	1	1" x 2½" x 62" (2.5 x 6.4 x 157.5 cm)
C	Back slats	11	½" x 2½" x 16' (1.3 x 6.4 cm x 4.8 m)
D	Front legs*	2	1¾" x 2½" x 9' (4.4 x 6.4 cm x 2.7 cm)
E	Back legs	2	1¾" x 5¼" x 6' (4.4 x 13.3 cm x 1.8 m)
F	Arms*	2	1¾" x 3½ ' x 4' (4.4 x 8.9 cm x 1.17 m)
G	Side seat rails*	2	1¾" x 2½" x 9' (4.4 x 6.4 cm x 2.7 cm)
H	Stretchers*	3	1¾" x 1¾" x 5' (4.4 x 4.4 cm x 150 cm)
I	Seat rails*	2	1¾" x 2½" x 9' (4.4 x 6.4 cm x 2.7 cm)
J	Seat slats	5	1" x 2½" x 6' (2.5 x 6.4 cm x 1.8 m)

* Length includes tenons

Smooth the edges and fair the curve by eye with 150-grit sandpaper.

3. Set a compass to 3½ inches (8.9 cm), and follow the sawn edge of the plywood with the tip of the compass to form the inner curve. Cut to this second line and sand as before, creating a template measuring 3½ inches (8.9 cm) wide.

4. Use the 36-inch-long (157.5 cm) plywood piece to make the template for the angled back leg (E). Starting at the bottom, narrow side of the plywood, mark a vertical line 17½ inches (44.5 cm) up and 2½inches (6.4 cm) in from the left side of the blank. From the 17½ 2 inch (44.5 cm) point, angle the line back approximately 8°, or until it intersects with the upper right-hand corner of the plywood blank, outlining the back, angled edge of the leg. Make a couple of marks 2½ inches (6.4 cm)

from the angled line, then connect the marks with a straightedge to draw the front angle.

Draw the 1-inch (2.5 cm) radiused curve on the upper back corner of the leg pattern by setting a compass to 1 inch (2.5 cm). Cut the leg template as before, using a jigsaw and smoothing the sawn edges with sandpaper. Set aside both leg and rail templates.

Building the Back

1. While the stock is still square, cut the tenons on the top back rail blank (A) and on the the bottom back rail (B) to the dimensions shown in fig. 2. You'll cut an oversize tenon on the top rail for now, then trim it later when you cut the curve in the rail. You can cut the tenons with a backsaw, or machine them on the table saw using a dado blade or a tenoning jig.

2. Lay out and clamp the top and bottom back rails (A and B), using a couple scrap boards exactly 12 inches (30.5 cm) long to seperate the two rails. Make sure the rails are square to each other.

3. Cut the 11 back slats (C) to rough length as shown in the cutting list, then position them beneath the top and bottom rails, spacing them equally, or about 2¾ (7 cm) apart. Mark the position of each slat onto the rails, then crosscut each slat 2 inches (5.1 cm) longer than its distance between the rails.

4. Unclamp the rails and cut the mortises for the slats. As shown in figures 2 and 3, size the mortises in the bottom rail to fit ¼-inch-thick (6 mm) tenons, and cut the mortises in the top rail ½ inch (1.3 cm) wide, or the full thickness of the back slats. Use a drill and

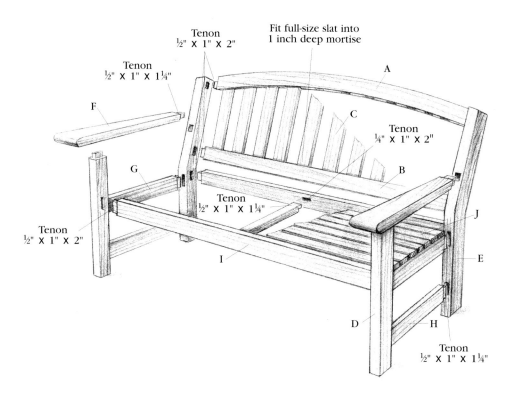

Tenon
½" X 1" X 2"

Tenon
½" X 1" X 1¼"

F

Fit full-size slat into
1 inch deep mortise

A

C

Tenon
¼" X 1" X 2"

B

G

Tenon
½" X 1" X 1¼"

Tenon
½" X 1" X 2"

I

J

E

D

H

Tenon
½" X 1" X 1¼"

Figure 2

¼- and ½-inch (6 mm and 1.3 cm) bits to drill the mortises, then chisel them square.

5. Cut the tenons on each slat's bottom end, as shown in fig.2. Leave the top of each slat full size.

6. Before assembling the back, find your plywood rail template, and trace its contours onto the top back rail blank (A). Cut the rail to its curved outline with a jigsaw or on the band saw. Clean up the sawn surfaces with a spokeshave or with sandpaper. Use a backsaw or the jigsaw to finish cutting the shoulder of the tenon on each end of the rail.

7. Dry-fit the back assembly, making any necessary adjustments. Then apply glue to all the joints and clamp the back together. To give the clamps purchase, you may need to place some

scrap wood blocks beneath the clamps along the top of the curved rail.

Making the Leg Assemblies

1. Cut the front and back legs (D and E), arms (F), side seat rails (G), and stretchers (H) to the dimensions shown in the cutting list. Dont cut the angles on the back leg or taper arms at this point.

2. Refer to figures 4 and 5 to lay out and cut the three mortises in each front leg (D) and the six mortises in each back leg (E). Compare your mortise layout in the back legs with the corresponding tenons you cut on the back assembly. Also lay out and cut the mortise in the underside of each arm, as shown in fig. 2. As before, drill and

then chisel the mortises square.

3. Cut the tenons on the front leg (D), the side seat rails (G), and the stretchers (H) to fit their corresponding mortises. You'll tenon the ends of the arms (F) later. Note that the tenons on the middle stretcher are offset and are flush to the top surface of the stretcher as shown in fig. 2.

4. Use the back leg template to trace the outline onto both back leg blanks (E), then saw the legs to shape with a jigsaw or on the band saw. Clean up any saw marks with a hand plane, spokeshave, or sandpaper.

5. Use a straightedge to lay out the taper on the arms (F), as shown in fig. 2. Then round over the front of each arm with a rasp, smoothing the end-grain curves with sandpaper.

6. Once you've shaped the arms, cut the angled tenon at the back of each arm as shown in fig. 2. Lay out the tenon with the bevel gauge set to the angle of the back leg, or 8°, then make the cheek and shoulder cuts by hand with the backsaw.

7. With all the parts cut and fitted, dry-clamp each side assembly to check for and correct any problems. When everything fits to your satisfaction, apply glue to all the joints and clamp each side assembly together. Use a square to check that the assemblies are square before setting them aside to dry.

Joining the Side and Back Assemblies

1. Before you can join the side and back assemblies, you'll need to cut the remaining frame pieces, the two seat rails (I), to the dimensions shown in the cutting list.

2. Lay out and cut a mortise in the center of each seat rail (I) as shown in fig. 2.

3. You're ready to assemble the bench frame. Apply glue to all the joints, fit the back and the two seat rails into one side assembly, then add the second side assembly. Use clamps to close all the joints, check for square, and leave the assembly to dry.

Adding the Seat Slats

1. Cut the five seat slats (J) to the dimensions shown. In the center and in the ends of each slat, counterbore, countersink, and drill #6 pilot holes through the slats for screws.

2. Position the slats so they are spaced equally across the side seat rails (G) and the middle stretcher (H), then secure the slats to the rails using three 2-inch (5.1 cm) screws per slat.

3. Now is the time to go over the entire bench with sandpaper, smoothing any irregularities and softening any sharp corners or arrises.

4. Finish up by plugging the screw holes with the wood plugs. Spread some glue on each plug, then tap it into the hole. When the glue has dried, pare the plugs flush with the bench seat using a razor-sharp chisel. Then apply a clear water sealer according to the package directions if you wish, or put the bench to use as it is.

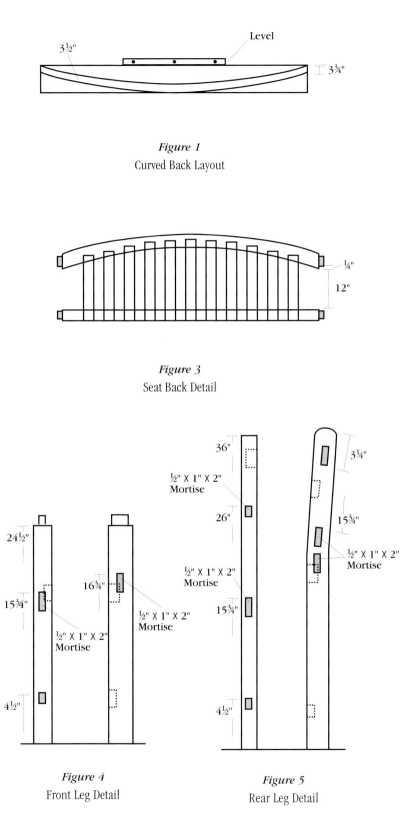

Figure 1
Curved Back Layout

Figure 3
Seat Back Detail

Figure 4
Front Leg Detail

Figure 5
Rear Leg Detail

NOTE: *For metric equivalents, refer to the chart on page 172*

LOW COUNTRY JOGGLE BENCH

*S*ome folks in the American South say the first bench of this type was built by a man in the 1800s for his elderly mother, who had arthritis and needed a little "bounce" to stand up from a seated position! Simple to build and fun to use, the long seat flexes when you sit on it. You can gently bounce up and down, or rock back and forth on the curved feet.

INSTRUCTIONS

Note: You can make the bench shorter if desired by decreasing the length of the seat (F). The longer the bench is, the more it will tend to "joggle" or bounce in use.

Making The Leg Assemblies

1. Cut out the four feet (A), four legs (B), and eight braces (C).

2. Set the base of the circular saw to a 45° angle and use it to miter both ends of each brace (C).

3. Referring to the dimensions in figures 1 and 2, lay out the curves at the bottom of the feet (A) and the gentle arches at the top of the legs (B). Use the scrap stick to generate the curves, or use the length of string with the pencil tied at one end to draw the radius. Saw to the layout lines with the jigsaw; cut from both sides of the stock if neccessary. Use the spokeshave or 150-grit sandpaper to smooth and fair the curves; smooth, bump-free curves on the feet will give a smoother rocking motion.

4. Lay out the three dowel hole locations in each leg (B) as shown in fig. 2. Drill the holes with a 1¼-inch (3.2 cm) spade bit, using the scrap block beneath the work to prevent tearout. Place a small square on the work as a guide to help you drill the holes square to the surface.

5. Make a centermark lengthwise on one side of one foot (A), and a corresponding centermark widthwise on the bottom side of one leg (B). Align the centermarks so the foot is centered on the leg, and clamp the foot and leg together.

6. Drill two 3/4-inch (1.9 cm), counter-bored holes in the bottom of the foot (A) in line with the leg (B). Drill the holes

about ⅜ inch (9.5 mm) deep, or deep enough to allow the head of a lag screw and a washer to recess into the foot. Then drill a ⅜-inch (9.5 mm) clearance hole into each counterbored hole, drilling through the foot (A) and ⅛ inch (3 mm) into the leg (B). Wrap a flag of masking tape around the bit to indicate the correct drilling depth.

7. Remove the clamp and the foot, and drill two 3/16-inch (4 mm) pilot holes into the end of the leg (B), using the shallow ⅜ inch (9 mm) holes to locate the bit. Drill the holes about 3 inches (7.6 cm) deep.

8. Attach the foot (A) to the leg (B) with two ⅜ x 7-inch (9.5 x 17.8 cm) lag screws and washers. Be sure that the heads of the lag screws don't protrude past the bottom face of the foot.

9. Position the two braces (C) on the leg assembly, with their corresponding miters snug against the foot (A) and the leg (B). Use the countersink and pilot bit to drill holes for screws. Secure each brace to the foot and the leg by driving a 1½-inch (3.8 cm) screw through each mitered end.

10. Repeat steps 5 through 9 to construct three more leg assemblies.

Assembling The Bench

1. Cut the six dowels (D) and the 12 pins (E) to length.

2. On each dowel (D), measure in ⅞ inch (2.2 cm) from each end, and drill ¼ inch (6mm) holes through the dowel. Keep the holes parallel with each dowel by clamping the stock on top of a scrap board, then eyeball a square placed near the dowel as you drill through the dowel and into the scrap.

3. Stand two leg assemblies upright and

approximately 12 inches (30.5 cm) apart, and insert a dowel (D) through each of the three holes in the legs (B). Let the dowels protrude about 1 inch (2.5 cm) beyond each leg. Now tap a pin (E) through each of the holes in the dowels with the hammer to lock the dowels in place. Align the dowels so the pins are level or parallel with the floor. To further strengthen the bottom dowel, drive a 2½-inch (6.4 cm) screw through each leg and into the dowel, toenailing at an angle through the leg and into the dowel. Repeat

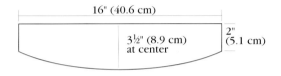

Figure 1

the assembly procedure with the remaining leg assemblies, dowels, pins and screws to make the second seat support.

4. Lay out and saw the curved ends on the seat (F) as shown in fig. 3. Refer to fig. 3 to locate the hole in each end of the bench, then use the 1-inch (2.5 cm) spade bit to drill the holes while using a backing block of scrap to prevent tearout.

5. Cut the two seat pins (G) to length. Use the block plane or spokeshave to taper the pins from 1¼ inch (3.2 cm) diameter at one end to ¾ inch (1.9 cm) at the opposite end. Use your fingers and eye to judge that the pins are round, then remove any tool marks and smooth them with 150-grit sandpaper.

6. As shown in figure 4, place the two bench supports about 9 feet (2.7 m) apart on the floor. Slide one end of the seat (F) between the top two dowels (D) of one support, until the hole in the seat is just past the dowels. Tap a seat pin (G) firmly

TOOLS

- Circular saw
- Jigsaw
- Small square
- Tape measure
- Spokeshave or block plane
- Power drill with Phillips #2 driver bit; #8 countersink and pilot bit; ⅜-inch, ¼-inch, $^{3}/_{16}$-inch (9.5 mm, 6 mm, 4.8 mm) drill bits; 1¼-inch, 1-inch, ¾-inch (3.2 cm, 2.54 cm, 1.9 cm) spade bits
- Bar-style clamps, 30 inches (76.2 cm)
- Hammer
- Paintbrush

HARDWARE AND SUPPLIES

- Scrap stick, ⅛" thick x 2' long, or nylon string (optional)
- Pencil
- 150-grit sandpaper
- Scrap wood block
- Masking tape
- 12 lag screws, ⅜ x 7 inches (9.5 mm x 17.8 cm) with washers
- 16 deck screws, #8 x 1½ inches (3.8 cm)
- 4 deck screws, #8 x 2½ inches (6.4 cm)
- Exterior-grade stain, oil-based enamel paint, or latex enamel paint

MATERIALS

1	1 x 2 x 8' fir
1	5/4 x 12 x 10' fir
2	4 x 4 x 8' fir
2	1¼ x 6' dowel (fir/pine)
1	¼ x 2' dowel (fir/pine)

CUTTING LIST

Code	Description	Qty.	Dimensions
A	Feet	4	3½ x 3½ x 16" (8.9 x 8.9 x 40.6 cm)
B	Legs	4	3½ x 3½ x 19" (8.9 x 8.9 x 53.34 cm)
C	Braces	8	¾ x 1½ x 8" (2.54 x 5.1 x 20.3 cm) from long point to long point of 45° miters
D	Dowels	6	1¼ x 21" (3.2 x 53.3 cm)
E	Dowel pins	12	¼ x 2" (6 mm x 5.1 cm)
F	Seat	1	1⅛ x 11¼" x 10' (2.85 cm x 30.5 cm x 3 m)
G	Seat pin	2	1¼ x 6" (3.2 x 15.2 cm)

into the hole in the seat. The dowel should extend roughly 2½ inches (6.4 cm) above the top of the seat.

7. Slide the free end of the seat (F) between the dowels (D) on the second support. Secure the seat in the same manner as before, driving the remaining seat pin (G) into the hole in the seat. With the seat in place, test its bounciness!

8. It's easier to apply a finish to the bench if you separate the assemblies. Remove the two seat pins to free the seat and the seat supports, and sand off any sharp edges or roughness. Wipe clean, and brush on the paint or stain. Let dry.

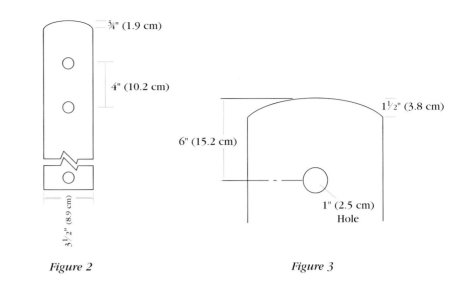

¾" (1.9 cm)

4" (10.2 cm)

3½" (8.9 cm)

Figure 2

1½" (3.8 cm)

6" (15.2 cm)

1" (2.5 cm) Hole

Figure 3

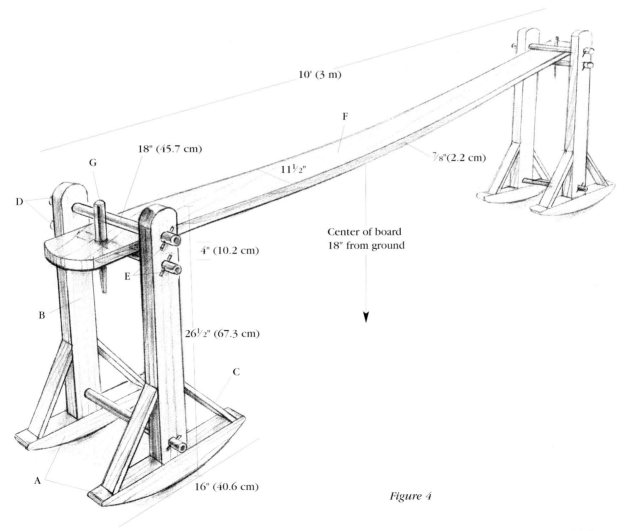

10' (3 m)

18" (45.7 cm)

G

F

11½"

⅞"(2.2 cm)

D

4" (10.2 cm)

E

Center of board 18" from ground

B

26½" (67.3 cm)

C

A

16" (40.6 cm)

Figure 4

Metal

Y ou don't have to be a working blacksmith with a forge to make metal garden furniture. With the right tools, you can easily work with recycled metal scrap, off-the-shelf materials, or prefabricated metal components such as the scrollwork that you'll trim and weld to make the Elegant Iron Chaise Lounge on page 131.

Simply put, metal is either ferrous (it has iron in it), or non-ferrous (it doesn't have iron in it). Steel is iron with extra carbon added. If sun heats it up, hose it down and cover it with a seat cushion. Metal is impervious to weather if you prime and paint it; touch up any corrosion annually with a rust-preventative paint, and scrub off moss with soap and water. You can also have metal powder-coated, an industrial process that

bakes on the paint for a very durable finish. Check the phone book for suppliers.

Precision is very important in metal projects. Unlike wood, metal can't easily be shaved down that extra quarter of an inch, so remember to measure twice before you cut! On the other hand, if you cut too much off a piece of iron or steel, you can just reweld the pieces together, remove any excess welding material with a grinder, and cut again.

Just like lumber, iron and steel are sold in assorted stock lengths and sizes, although the shapes are more varied: ½-inch (1.3 cm) round rod, ½-inch (1.3 cm) square rod, ¼-inch (6 mm) flat bar, and 1-inch (2.5 cm) round tubing, for example. You buy metal by the linear foot, or by the piece if it's a prefabricated component. You can purchase iron and steel stock from local industrial suppliers and metal distributors. Prefabricated parts can be ordered by mail from ornamental iron suppliers. Many welding shops will gladly supply both stock and components.

You can do a great deal of metalwork with a vise and a hacksaw, but you can also simply take the parts for your project to a weld shop or metal fabricator for extensive cutting or welding.

Painting and Sealing Metal

Metal is a beautiful material in itself. You may simply want to knock off the larger pieces of rust with a wire brush, then put a coat of sealer on to arrest the oxidation process.

Before painting metal, it's important to prepare the surface. Remove every bit of rust with a wire brush and sanding blocks, then clean the surface with soap and water. If the surface has a lacquered finish (if you can remove flakes with the straight edge of a razor blade, it's there), sand off the lacquer with fine steel wool dipped in denatured alcohol. Clean again

This forged steel bench was painted with interior latex paint so it would rust and acquire an "aged" patina. Hays Cash Design, 1999.

PHOTO BY REED PHOTOGRAPHY

Below: Nancy Owens, *Fire Escape Bench*, dimensions various; steel; cut, welded, painted. Nancy Owens, Landscape Architect, New York, NY

with soap and water, then scouring powder, and finish by wiping it down with denatured alcohol or another solvent. The repeated sanding and scouring may seem like overkill, but these processes create tooth on the surface that will grab and hold the paint better.

Paint the dry metal with rust-inhibiting metal primer, and let it dry. Brush on exterior-grade paint. The primer and paint must be chemically compatible, either oil-based or acrylic (water) based. Acrylic is easier to clean up, but oil-based paint provides better, more durable protection. After the final coat of paint dries, brush or spray on a couple of coats of clear sealer for more protection against the elements.

You can use artist's brushes to paint freehand designs on the surface, or use stencils. Buy a stencil brush and ready-made stencils at craft stores, or make the stencils yourself. Try tracing leaves from plants in your garden onto a piece of thin cardboard, acetate, or blank stencil material, then cut away the inside with a craft knife. Lay the stencil on the metal surface and spray, sponge, or brush on paint. You can also use leaves or other other objects as "reverse stencils," laying them on the surface and spraying around the perimeter, leaving a pretty ghost image. Let dry, and finish with clear sealer.

MATERIALS

Metal lawn chair

Rust-resistant acrylic spray primer

Acrylic spray paint in light yellow, olive green, and khaki

Acrylic craft paint in several shades of green, including teal and forest

1 roll each of painter's tape in 1- and 2-inch (2.5 and 5.1 cm) widths

Clear acrylic spray sealer

TOOLS AND SUPPLIES

Wire brush

Sandpaper

Rag

Ruler or tape measure

Pencil

Carpenter's square

Foam brushes in assorted sizes

Foam stamps in maple leaf and fern designs

FLORAL PLAID LAWN CHAIR

DESIGNER
JEAN TOMASO MOORE

Down-home garden seating meets fine decorating in this wonderful chair! Easily applied acrylic paint, tape, and foam stamps reproduce a classic leaf-and-plaid pattern. With this project, you can renovate even the shabbiest metal lawn chair.

Some of your lawn chairs may be such old friends, you'd never think of altering them! You might even give them a pet name.

INSTRUCTIONS

1. Prepare the surface of the chair by using the wire brush to remove all rust and loose paint. Sand down the chair to create as smooth a finish as possible, then dampen the rag and wipe away surface debris.

2. Following the directions on the can, spray on several coats of the primer and allow to dry.

3. Select one of the lighter shades from your color palette of acrylic spray paints, and spray on two coats to serve as the base color. (Yellow was used for the base coat of the chair pictured.) Let dry overnight.

4. With the ruler or tape measure, find the center point on the back of the chair. Use the carpenter's square to draw a vertical pencil line along the center of the entire chair, including the seat, back, and backside.

5. Apply the 2-inch (5.1 cm) painter's tape along the center of the pencil line, running a line of tape over the seat, the back, over the back, and down the backside of the chair. Press the tape firmly in place, being especially careful with the edges.

6. With the ruler, measure points approximately 2 inches (5.1 cm) on both sides of the tape. Following the points, use the carpenter's square and pencil to draw parallel lines on the chair. Apply the 2-inch (5.1 cm) tape along the center of the newly drawn lines.

7. Decide how you'll space the first set of horizontal lines. Their spacing

doesn't have to be uniform, but use the ruler to keep the lines straight and square. Mark the lines in pencil, and put the 1-inch (2.5 cm) tape on top to form the horizontal pattern. Press the tape down firmly, ensuring the edges are secure.

8. Spray the chair with the khaki spray paint or another color of similar tone. Leave the tape in place and allow to dry.

9. With the original taping still on the chair (and masking the lightest color), tape the chair again both horizontally and vertically with 1-inch (2.5 cm) tape. Apply the tape in an alternative pattern. Place two to three strips of tape in each direction to create the initial plaid.

10. With the tape firmly in place, spray the chair with the third and darkest color, olive. While the paint is still wet, peel off the layers of tape one piece at a time to reveal the masked colors underneath. On this chair, the original taping masked the yellow, the second masked the khaki, and the top layer was the olive green.

11. To add additional colors to the plaid, apply more tape in vertical and horizontal patterns, and use the foam brushes to apply other shades of acrylic craft paints. Peel the tape off when the paint is still wet, but allow each color to dry before adding additional tapings.

12. When you're satisfied with your plaid design, use a small paintbrush to touch up any messy edges.

13. Use one of the foam brushes to apply the acrylic craft paints to the foam leaf and fern stamps. Layer leaf prints onto the chair in various shades of green and blue-green. Press the stamp firmly against the chair, and pull it cleanly away to prevent smearing.

14. When you've applied all the stamped images you desire and the paint has dried, spray on several coats of the clear acrylic spray to seal and protect the chair.

Elegant Iron Chaise Lounge

DESIGNERS

Doug Hays and Penny Cash

Y*ou don't have to be a master blacksmith to create this gorgeous lounge chair! Its fabulous flourishes and curlicues are actually ready-made scrollwork used for gates and railings, and you can buy them from ornamental iron suppliers. The other metal stock you need is easily found from the same sources, or through steel distributors. If you've never welded before, take the parts to a local welding shop.*

MATERIALS

14 feet (4.2 m) of ½-inch (1.3 cm) round, hot-rolled, mild steel

31 feet (9.3 m) of 2½- x ¼-inch (6.4 cm x 6mm) flat, hot-rolled, mild steel

6 pieces of metal scrollwork with a curlicue on each end, each piece 28⅜ inches (72.1 cm) long and 9⅞ inches wide*

4 pieces of metal scrollwork with a curlicue on each end and in the middle section, each piece 28⅜ inches long and 9⅞ inches (25.1 cm) wide*

2 finials*, 3⅞ inches (5.2 cm) tall

*You can mail-order scrollwork and finials from metal fabricators and suppliers to architectural firms, or order them through a local welding shop.

TOOLS AND SUPPLIES

Large work table or clear floor area, 5 x 10 feet (1.5 x 3 m)

Fine-tip permanent marker

Vise

Hacksaw

Piece of chalk

Piece of string, 8 feet (2.4 m) long

Tape measure

Miter saw with abrasive blade, or chop saw

Welding equipment (optional)

Paintbrush

Primer for steel, spray-on or in a can

Exterior-grade paint for steel, spray-on or in a can

INSTRUCTIONS

1. Lay out the pieces on the table or floor. Set aside the two "S" scrolls, which you'll cut apart later. Roughly arrange the scrolls as shown in fig. 1. Prefabricated scrollwork often has slightly inconsistent dimensions, and you may have to bend it a little to make it fit.

2. Take the two "S" scrolls you put aside earlier, and fit them in the laid-out pieces. Use the marker to indicate where they need to be cut (see fig. 2). Secure a scroll in the vise, cut it with the hacksaw, and add the piece to the layout. Repeat with the second scroll.

3. As shown in fig. 1, the two pieces of ½-inch (1.3 cm) round stock that run the length of the lounge on both sides will form the support for the slats. In turn, the arrangement of the scrollwork determines the contour of the slat support. You'll make two bends in each support by hand, with the support anchored in the vise. You may also choose to have a local weld shop make the bends for you.

When you plan where you'll make the bends, the backrest should be at least 30 inches (76.2 cm) high to allow you to lean your head back and take a nap! A comfortable angle for reclining is 22 to 30°. Allow 19 to 21 inches (48.3 to 53.34 cm) of the seat to support your rear and thighs, and 26 inches (66 cm) for your lower legs. With these "comfort parameters" in mind, use the chalk to draw a line on your work surface along the top of the scrollwork. The line should touch most of the ironwork. Measure the length of the line by running the piece of string along it, then measure the string.

4. Secure a piece of the ½-inch (1.3 cm) round stock in the vise, and use the abrasive blade on the miter saw or the chop saw to cut it to the length of the string plus at least 12 more inches (30.5 cm). Measure and mark where the first bend will be. When bending metal bar, it's best to bend in increments instead of one big effort, which is harder and may torque the metal. Clamp the round stock into the vise again, give it a slight bend, and check it against the scrollwork layout to make sure it's achieving the necessary shape. If so, bend it a little bit more until it forms the desired angle. Make the second bend but don't trim the piece yet. Repeat with the second piece of ½-inch (1.3 cm) round stock. Lay out both pieces against the scrollwork, and mark where they need to be trimmed. Trim them with the power tool, or put them aside for the weld shop to cut.

5. Now you'll cut the slats from the 2-½-inch x ¼-inch (6.4 cm x 6 mm) flat stock. The slats are 19 inches (48.3 cm) long and are spaced about 1 inch (2.5 cm) apart. In the photo, the last two slats following the scrollwork are 2 inches (5.1 cm) wide. Don't waste your time trying to cut the slats without power tools. Use the miter saw with the abrasive blade, or the chop saw, to cut them, or take the stock to a metal fabricator to be cut.

6. At this point, if you haven't welded before, take the parts to a local welding shop. With the scrollwork still lying flat on the work surface or floor, tack-weld it together to form the two sides of the lounge. While everything is still flat, weld the side supports onto the scrollwork. Stand each side upright and temporarily brace them. Now you'll weld on the slats. Make sure the two sides

are square, plumb, level, and the right distance apart, using a slat as a spacer. Weld the pieces together with permanent welds, starting at the bottom and working your way up.

7. Weld the two finials to the upper ends of the seat supports.

8. Paint the metal with the primer, paying close attention to the nooks and crannies. Allow to dry, then paint with the exterior-grade metal paint.

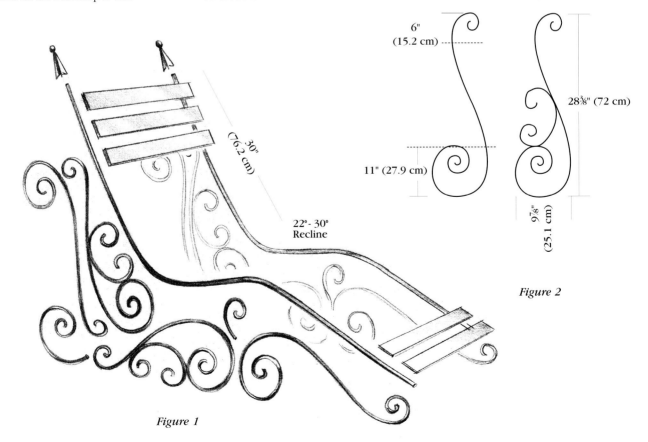

30"
(76.2 cm)

22°- 30°
Recline

6"
(15.2 cm)

28⅜" (72 cm)

11" (27.9 cm)

9⅞"
(25.1 cm)

Figure 2

Figure 1

Sparky, the Three-Legged Chair

DESIGNER
Cynthia Wynn

*T*his contemporary chair combines copper wire, rebar, and recycled roofing tin in an inventive design that doesn't require welding. Curled feet and elegant curves add graceful and whimsical elements, topped by spark plugs used as decorative accents!

MATERIALS

6 lengths of #3 rebar, 10 feet (3 m) each

Salvaged roofing tin, enough to make one triangle

3 x 3 x 1½ foot (0.9 x0.9 m x 45.7 cm) and one triangle

1 x 1 x 1 foot (0.9 x 0.9 x 0.9 m)

48 feet (14.4 m) of large-gauge copper wire*

50 feet (15 m) of 16-gauge copper wire

25 feet (7.5 m) of 20-gauge copper wire

4 spark plugs

*Copper wire salvaged from 220 electrical cable works perfectly.

TOOLS AND SUPPLIES

Safety glasses

Protective gloves

Tape measure

Fine-tip permanent marker

Bench vise

A helpful friend

Bolt cutters

Sharp utility knife

Small, handheld propane torch

Lighter or striker

Hammer

Chipping hammer

Cable cutters

Needle-nose pliers

Needle-nose vise grips

Regular vise grips

Large jaw vise grips

2 C-clamps, 3- to 6-inch (7.6 cm to 15.2 cm) size, depending on the width of your workbench

Piece of flat bar, 24 inches (61 cm) long

1-inch (2.5 cm) pipe, 3 feet (.9 m) long

Pipe bender

Hand punch or awl

Poster board

Scissors

Fast-drying spray paint

Tin snips, or a high speed drill with a hummer wheel

Sandpaper or synthetic scouring pad

Rag

Solvent

Semigloss wood lacquer

Paintbrush

INSTRUCTIONS

1. You should always wear safety glasses and protective gloves when working with metal or wire, so put them on. First, you'll create the decorative curls for the back and feet of the chair. The two back legs will have curls 5 inches (12.7 cm) in diameter, and the four legs will have curls 2½ inches (6.4 cm) in diameter. Cold-bending rebar into small shapes is challenging, and you'll find it helpful to have a friend to assist

you with this step. Use the tape measure and marker to mark all six lengths of rebar at a point 4 feet, 5 inches (1.2 m, 12.7 cm) from one end.

2. One at a time, clamp each length of rebar in the bench vise with the short end pointing down and the mark at the top of the vise jaws. Grip the long end of the bar close to the vise jaws and pull down, bending the bar into an approximate 45° angle as shown in fig. 1.

3. Remove the bar from the vise, and reclamp its long end into the vise with the bottom of the V-shape pointing up. Pull the short end of the bar up until you have a curl like the one in fig. 2.

4. Use the bolt cutters to trim the short end off the curl, cutting at a point about ¾ inch (1.9 cm) before the crossover point.

5. Repeat the process of clamping and curling on the opposing end of the bar to make the second, duplicate curl for the back. As you bend the second curl, it's important to bend up on the opposite side of the long end of the bar, so that when the curl is trimmed and laid side by side with the other bar for the back, the curls match but the bars go out in opposite directions, as shown in fig. 3.

6. Repeat steps 2 through 5 to make all four legs.

7. Have your friend help you with this stage. One by one, clamp the curl of each leg in the bench vise and simultaneously pull out and down, tightening the curl into a 2½-inch (6.4 cm) circle. At least two of the leg curls are mirror opposites, like the back curls.

8. Use the bolt cutters to trim off the short ends of the foot curls about ¾ inch (1.9 cm) from the crossover points.

9. Salvage the wire from the 220 cable by using the cable cutters to cut the cable into twenty-four 2-foot (.6 m) sections. Slice the casing open with the knife to free the individual wires, then strip them of their insulation by slicing lengthwise with the knife.

10. Hammer both ends of the 24 pieces of wire to flatten them.

11. Large-gauge wire is stiff and difficult to bend, but you can anneal the wires, softening them by heating each one until it's red hot. Light the propane torch with the lighter, and use it to heat each wire. Allow the wires to cool. If the wire becomes work-hardened again as you work with it, anneal it again so it's malleable.

Making the Chair Frame Back

12. Now you'll make the back of the chair frame. Use the pipe bender to curve the two pieces of rebar intended for the back, starting at the curl and ending halfway down. Bend the two bars to match each other as shown in fig. 4.

13. Use the annealed copper wire to lash together the two rebar curls. Put the flattened end of the wire between the curls, and clamp the curls together with the bench vise. Hammer the flat end of the wire that's sticking out so it wraps around the rebar.

14. Begin wrapping the wire around both pieces of the rebar, keeping tension on the wire with your hands or by clamping the needle-nose vise grips to the wire's end when possible. To ensure a tight lashing, pinch and twist the wire with the needle-nose pliers, and after each wrap, tap the wire into the space between the rebar with the chipping hammer.

Making the Back Brace

15. Make the brace for the back of the chair by taking one of the short pieces of rebar (left over from the bar you trimmed after making the curl), clamping it in the table vise, and bending a U-shaped cross support. Bend the U so it's slightly uneven to give the chair a more jaunty air. The U-shaped bracket will be 14 inches (35.6 cm) across; where its bend stops, there will be two 10-inch (25.4 cm) lengths. See figure 5.

16. Trim off the excess rebar with the bolt cutters, leaving straight, 10-inch (25.4 cm) lengths at the ends of the U.

17. Using the flat bar and two C-clamps, clamp the V to the work table, leaving the 10-inch (25.4 cm) lengths sticking out. Slip a 3-foot (.9 m) section of the 1-inch (2.5 cm) pipe over a 10-inch (25.4 cm) section of the rebar to provide extra leverage, and bend the section up into a right angle. The brace should now look like fig. 6.

18. Spread apart the two free ends of the lashed-together back section so that the U-shaped brace fits between them at the end of the curved portion of the back. The 10-inch (25.4 cm) sections of the brace should stick straight out behind the chair back. Clamp the back and the brace together, and lash them together tightly with the annealed wire. Use the lashing technique described in step 14 at this point, and at all other points where required.

19. Use the pipe bender to bend together the remaining portions of the back toward each other. Cross them at a point about 10 inches (25.4 cm) from their ends, and lash together securely with the annealed copper wire.

20. Now you'll bend the bottom half of the chair back so it matches the top half. Use the C-clamps to clamp the entire piece face down on the worktable, placing the bar directly under the U-shaped brace. The 10-inch (25.4 cm) pieces will be sticking up. Grasp the crossed section and push up. Move the bar down 4 inches (10.2 cm) and push up again, repeating the process until you've achieved the desired curve. See figure 7.

Making and Attaching the Legs

21. To create the chair's back leg, repeat steps 12 and 13. Then, starting from the curl, bend a curve halfway up each bar as shown in fig. 8. Lash the two curls together to form one back foot.

22. With the curls pointing down, attach the back foot piece to the chair back. The foot should be positioned under the crossed portion of the chair back. The curled portion of the back foot piece will be positioned outside the crossed ends of the chair back, and the two "arms" of the foot piece will pass under the two curved corners of the U-shaped brace at the inside of the chair back. Lash the back foot section to the chair back in four places as shown in fig. 9: two by the crossed portion of the

1

2

3

4

(35.6 cm)
14 "

5

(25.4 cm)
10 "

6

7

chair back and two to the right angles of the U-shaped brace.

23. You'll use the the two straight pieces of the back foot section to create the front leg supports. Clamp as necessary and bend each piece down, curving them to point backward toward the back foot (see fig. 10).

24. You'll use the two remaining pieces of curled rebar to construct the front legs. Take a bar and put its curl in the vise. Bend back against the curl to accent the fiddlehead shape of the front feet. Refer to fig. 11. Repeat with the second bar.

25. Use the tape measure and marker to indicate a point 18 inches (45.7 cm) from the bottom of the curl. Clamp the bar in the vise with the curl pointing down, and bend a right angle at that point. Measure and mark a point 16 inches (40.6 cm) from the front of the right angle. Reclamp, and bend another angle that's not quite as sharp. With the bolt cutters, cut the remaining rebar off 12 inches (30.5 cm) from the middle of the second angle. Bend the 12-inch (30.5 cm) portion back to match the curve of the chair back.

26. As shown in fig. 12, bend the ends of the front leg support so they fit into the heel of the front leg piece. With the bolt cutters, trim off about 7½ inches (19.1 cm).

(40.6 cm)
16 "

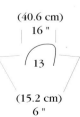

(15.2 cm)
6 "

27. Lash the front legs to the chair at four points on each leg: two at the back of the chair, one at the seat, and one at the heel of the front foot. Cross the 12-inch (30.5 cm) portions of the front

legs behind the back of the chair, splaying out the front legs to make the chair more stable. Check the stability of the chair as you lash on the front legs, adjusting as necessary.

28. The U-shaped brace for the front is the last piece you'll bend. Repeat steps 15 through 17, achieving the profile shown in figs. 13 and 6. This U-brace will measure 16 inches (40.6 cm) across and 10 inches (25.4 cm) long. Bend it a little unevenly to give the chair design character!

29. Fit the front brace between the two front legs, and lash it in two places on each side. You've now completed the chair frame.

Making and Attaching the Seat

30. Use the poster board and marker to make patterns of the inside areas of the chair seat and back, and cut out the patterns with the scissors. Lay the patterns on the salvaged roofing tin, and use fast-drying spray paint around the pattern edges to mark the area you'll cut.

31. Cut out the tin with the snips, or secure the tin with the clamps and cut it with the hummer wheel on the drill. Be careful, the edges are sharp! Check the fit of the tin to the chair frame and trim any excess.

32. Use the sandpaper or synthetic scouring pad to smooth the edges of the tin and remove any burrs.

33. Use the hand punch or the awl and hammer to make holes every 3 inches (7.6 cm) around the edge of the tin, ⅜ inch (9.5 mm) from the edge.

34. Wire the tin to the frame with the 16-gauge copper wire. Use the wire snips to cut two pieces of wire per hole. Thread the wire through the tin and around the rebar frame, twisting the ends of the wire together with the needle-nose vise grips to ensure a tight connection. Hide the twisted ends under or behind the chair.

35. For a fun finishing touch, use the 20-gauge copper wire to wire the spark plugs to the raw ends of rebar that stick out in the chair back. First, lash the wire around the rebar and the plugs, then tighten them by lashing between the rebar and plugs.

36. Wipe the chair with the rag and solvent to remove any dirt or grease. Let dry, and finish it by applying the semigloss wood lacquer with the brush.

Chapter VIII

FABRIC

The main disadvantage of using fabric outdoors is the need to protect it from the elements. Sun fades cloth, and moisture leads to decay. It helps to use 100 percent synthetic fabric, to spray the fabric with water repellent, to seal fabric accessories with clear vinyl, and to shelter it from rain and sun. You can also purchase more expensive, heavy fabrics designed to be used in outdoor applications, such as patio furniture, but you'll need a heavy-duty sewing machine. The best response may be to use fabric in casual projects that aren't too labor intensive, so you'll feel fine about replacing it with something new after a few seasons.

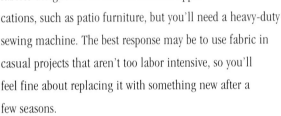

You can easily sew covers for plastic deck chairs that are trim and tailored, or lush and romantic as a fairytale.

Before You Start Sewing ...

Yes, you can paint plastic deck chairs if you choose, rather than cover them. First, clean the surface very well, using vinegar and water or a commercial degreaser. Sand lightly to remove the gloss from the surface, then remove any dust with a tack cloth. Spray-paint the chair with primer, let dry, then spray again with the color of your choice. You can also use paint that already contains primer. You may have to apply more than one coat of paint to achieve an even finish.

Fabric

You have an enormous variety of colors and prints available in woven cloth to use for outdoor seating. You can also use plain fabric as a ground for your own decoration (see the sponge-painted floral treatment of the Director's Chairs in Bloom on page 148). You can also stuff fabric with batting, and quilt it with a simple machine stitch, to create glorious, sculptural creations like the Giant Hibiscus Pillows on page 162. They're big enough to sit in!

Unless you enjoy leisurely hand sewing, you'll need a sewing machine. Fabric is easy to work with, particularly in projects that don't require much more than sewing straight seams. Simplify your efforts by avoiding projects that require zippers or elaborately constructed corners and edges. For truly no-hassle, slip-on pillow covers, see the instructions included with the Plastic Deck Chair Covers on page 142.

Fabric is available in widths ranging from 20 to 60 inches (50.8 to 152.4 cm) or wider. If you're using a print such as a plaid, and you want the pattern to match at the seams, buy an extra ½ yard (.45 m) to give you some extra "wiggle" room in placing the pattern pieces. When you cut out the pieces, be sure to allow for ½-inch (1.3 cm) seams along all the edges to be sewn. When you make pillows or other small, fabric-covered accessories for the outdoors, it's a perfect opportunity to

recycle the fabric from old clothing or worn linens.

MATERIALS

2 yards (1.8 m) of 45-inch (114.3 cm) linen-weave fabric or coarse, tightly woven cotton fabric in gray or taupe

4 packages of ½-inch (1.3 cm), prefolded bias binding tape, 3 yards (2.7 m) each, in white

Selection of grosgrain ribbon in different widths and shades of blue, each piece at least 15 inches (38.1 cm) long

Thread in colors to match the fabric, bias binding, and ribbons

6 grommets, 1½-inch (3.8 cm) diameter*

6 large screw-in hooks

Trio of wooden stools

*Contact custom awning manufacturers, patio furniture suppliers, or marine distributors to obtain oversize grommets. They can also install the grommets in the pillows for you.

TOOLS AND SUPPLIES

Tape measure

Chalk

Scissors

Straight pins

Sewing machine

Needle

Polyester filling

Grommet setter (optional)

Hammer (optional)

Rubber pad, or wad of newspapers (optional)

GROMMET PILLOW SEAT SETS

This clever project is a good reason to get all hung up about outdoor seating! The oversize grommets and graphic ribbon trim make these pillows both stylish and fun. Try combining them with mismatched stools from your local flea market.

INSTRUCTIONS

1. Open up the fabric. Use the tape measure, chalk, and scissors to measure, mark, and cut out 12 squares from the fabric. Each square should measure 15 inches (38.1 cm) square, which includes ½-inch (1.3 cm) seam allowances. The finished pillows will measure 14 inches (35.6 cm) square.

2. Pin the decorative ribbon to the right sides of six of the squares, in designs that please you. These will form the fronts of the pillows. Sew the ribbons in place by using the machine to stitch along both edges.

3. Pin a decorated square and a plain square together, right side out, and hand-baste a ½-inch (1.3 cm) seam around the margins. Leave a 3- or 4-inch (7.6 or 10.2 cm) opening on one side of a corner. This is where you'll insert the polyester stuffing later. Remove the pins.

4. Open up the bias binding tape slightly. Starting at the corner where

you left the opening (but not covering the opening), slip the tape over the raw edges of the pillow with the widest side of the tape on the underside of the pillow. Pin the tape in place along three sides. Leave a long tail of the tape free on the fourth and final side, so you can finish the corner after you've stuffed the pillow.

5. Topstitch the tape in place, folding the corners into place as you work. When your seam approaches a corner, tuck excess tape underneath the corner, much like wrapping the corners of a package. Stop sewing before you close up the opening in the seam.

6. Insert the polyester stuffing loosely into the pillow. Pin the remaining binding tape in place, trimming it with the scissors and tucking under the raw end of the tape to create the final, lapped corner. Finish machine-sewing the seam. Remove the pins and any visible basting. Repeat steps 2 through 6 to construct the remaining five pillows.

7. Following package directions, use the grommet setter and hammer to install a pair of grommets on three of the pillows, working on top of the rubber pad or newspapers. You may also choose to take the pillows to a custom awning manufacturer or other industrial vendor to have them install the grommets.

8. Set the stools in position against the wall where they'll "live." Use the ruler and pencil to make two marks on the wall about 22 inches (55.9 cm) above the stool seats and 12 inches (30.5 cm) apart (the distance from center to center of two grommets). Use the level to verify that the two marks are level.

9. Screw in a hook at each mark. Hang three pillows from the hooks, and place the other pillows on the seats underneath.

MATERIALS

Plastic deck chair

2½ yards (2.25 m) of fabric, which includes 2 yards (1.8 m) for the chair and ½ yard (.45 m) for a 1 x 15 x 17-inch (2.5 x 38.1 x 43.2 cm) seat cushion*

½ yard (.45m) of cotton polyester broadcloth to line the seat cushion (optional)

16-ounce (448 g) bag of polyester stuffing

Plastic stool to match the deck chair (optional)

Piece of fabric for the stool cover, approximately 48 (1.2 m) x 55 inches (1.38 m) (optional)

½ yard (.45 m) of fabric for the stool cushion (optional)

Foam cushion form to fit the top of the stool (optional)

*Based on the dimensions of the chair shown in fig. 1, a 40-inch-wide (3 m) fabric will leave about 5 inches (12.7 cm) of the chair legs showing. A 54-inch-wide (1.35 m) fabric will cover the chair to the floor, and a 60-inch-wide (4.5 m) fabric will reach the floor and allow a lush, full effect. If you wish to use 54-inch-wide (1.5 m) white cotton gauze like one of the chairs shown, buy 4½ yards (4.05 m) because it will look best if you use a double layer of material.

TOOLS AND SUPPLIES

Tape measure

Piece of chalk

Scissors

Straight pins

Sewing machine

Thread to match fabric

Electric iron

Pencil

DECK CHAIR COVERS WITH MATCHING CUSHIONS AND HASSOCK

DESIGNER
JANE WILSON

⊙kay, time for a reality check! Admit it, we all have some plastic deck chairs on our patio or stored in the garage. But if you can sew a straight seam, you can make these attractive slipcovers in minutes (and save lots of money compared to pricey store-bought covers). You can also make an elegant hassock out of a plastic stool, and slip-on cushion covers using a very simple technique that doesn't require zippers, welting, or other complicated construction.

INSTRUCTIONS

Making the Chair Cushion

1. First, you'll make the cover. Calculate the desired dimensions of the finished cushion, remembering to include the thickness of the cushion and seam allowances in your length and width measurements. For example, the finished cushion shown in the blue plaid chair measures 17 x 15 inches (43.2 x 38.1 cm) and is 1 inch (2.5 cm) thick. Therefore, the fabric was cut in a 19 x 32-inch (48.3 x 81.28 cm) piece. Seventeen inches (43.2 cm) plus two ½-inch (1.3 cm) seams, plus the thickness of the finished cushion, equals 19 inches (48.3 cm). Two 15-inch (38.1 cm) sides, plus two ½-inch (1.3 cm) seam allowances, plus 1 inch (2.5 cm) for the thickness, equals 32 inches (81.28 cm). Use the tape measure and chalk to measure and mark a piece of the fabric to the correct size, and cut it out with the scissors. If you think your fabric should be lined, cut a piece of the lining fabric the same size and pin it to the wrong side of the fabric, then proceed as directed below, treating the pinned pieces as one piece.

2. Right sides together, sew the edges together with a ½-inch (1.3 cm) seam, leaving a 6-inch (15.2 cm) opening to insert the polyester filling.

3. Now you'll create the two front corners of the seat cushion by using the same technique shown in figure 6 of the Bench Cushion instructions on page 159. With the cover still wrong side out, twist the fabric diagonally at one corner, so that the raw edge of one of the short seams is centered in the corner. Pin together, and use the tape

measure to measure in from the corner, along the centered seam, the same distance as the thickness of the cushion insert. Sew a seam at that point, inside the corner, from one side of the corner to the other. Remove the pins. Repeat with the other corner and short seam. Use the scissors to trim excess material from the corners. You can leave the two rear corners of the cushion unstructured.

4. Turn the cover right side out. Stuff with the polyester filling. Make sure the raw edges of the opening are tucked inside, and sew it shut.

Making the Chair Cover

1. The chair cover is constructed much like an oversize pillowcase. Fold the remaining 2 yards (1.8 m) of fabric right side together, pinning the short edges (A) together with the straight pins. Thread the machine, and sew ½-inch (1.3 cm) seams along the short edges (A). Lightly press the seams open with the iron.

If you're working with white cotton gauze, you'll want to use a double layer of the material for the best effect. Refer to figure 3. Take a 4-yard (3.6 m) piece of the gauze, fold crossways, and pin together the ends (A). Sew a ½-inch (1.3 cm) seam (B) and remove the pins (fig. 2). Turn the material so the seam is inside (fig. 3), and fold the gauze in the same direction again (fig. 4) so the folded edge (C) meets the seamed edge (B). Pin each of the sides (D), and sew a ½-inch (1.3 cm) seam on each end (fig. 5).

1. Check the measurements of the stool as shown in figure 7. Add 1 extra inch (2.5 cm) to the length and 1 extra inch (2.5 cm) to the breadth to allow for a hem.

2. Take the piece of fabric and fold it as shown in figure 8, marking the center point with a straight pin.

3. Use the measuring tape to determine the center point of the stool and mark it with the pencil. Spread the fabric over the stool, right side down, matching the pin to the center. Smooth the fabric over the stool, and use pins to mark all four corner points of the top.

4. Keeping the fabric centered on the stool, pin the excess fabric at the four corners of the stool (see fig. 9). Use the tape measure to make sure you've pinned the fabric to the same depth at each corner and adjust if necessary. Mark the pinned corner edges with the

2. Turn the cover right side out. (Note: the rest of this step isn't necessary for a gauze cover.) Turn ¼ inch (6 mm) of the raw edge of fabric to the inside, then another ½ inch (1.3 cm) under again. Use the iron to press the creases. Use the machine to topstitch a seam over the folded edge to keep the hem in place. Press again if desired.

3. Refer to fig. 6. Open up the chair cover, and lower it over the chair back to encase the chair. You'll know you have it positioned correctly when the seams fall along the chair arms at a point about 4 or 5 inches (10.2 or 12.7 cm) along the curve of the arms, and then flow to each side of the chair and to the ground. Arrange the length and drape of the cover to your liking. Where the chair back meets the seat, use your fingers to make a horizontal pleat at the back of the seat, folding in any

excess fabric. Drop in the seat cushion to hold everything in place, with the sewn-in corners at the front of the chair.

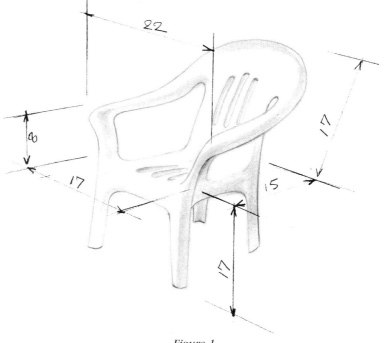

Figure 1

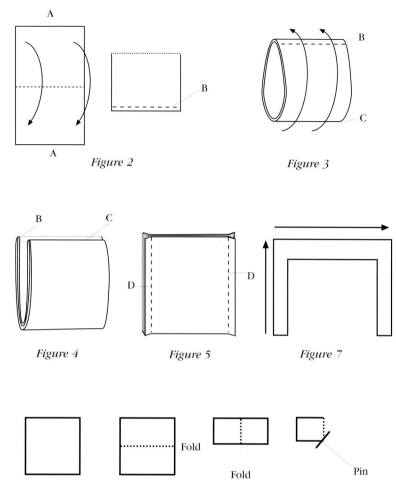

Figure 2

Figure 3

Figure 4

Figure 5

Figure 7

 Fold

Fold

 Pin

Figure 8

chalk, if desired, for a visual aid.

5. Lift the pinned cover off the stool, and use the machine to sew a seam along each pinned and chalked line. With the scissors, trim the excess fabric from the seams.

6. Along the raw edge of the cover's hem, turn a ½-inch (1.3 cm) edge of the fabric to the inside, then fold it over again. Press with the iron to sharpen the crease. Sew a seam on top of the folded margin, all the way around, to create a hem.

7. Turn the cover right side out, and fit it over the stool.

8. If you'd like to top the stool with a cushion, follow the directions for the Bench Cushion on page 158, adapting them to an insert sized for the stool top.

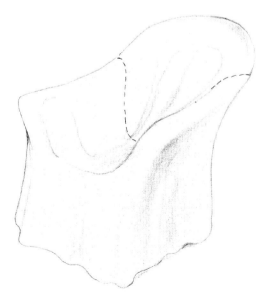

Figure 6

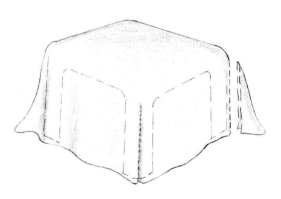

Figure 9

MATERIALS

Old poster on heavy stock, or images from magazines, wrapping paper, or calendars

Heavy paper, 21 x 18 inches (53.34 x 45.7 cm)

Piece of bright-colored vinyl, at least 20 x 23 inches (50.8 x 58.4 cm)

TOOLS AND SUPPLIES

White glue

Ruler

Permanent fine-tip marker or pencil

Craft knife or scissors

Masking tape

Sewing machine, or needle and thread

Pinking shears

Awl or ice pick

Package of plastic lacing or braiding material* or butcher's string

*Available at craft stores

WOVEN SIT-UPON

DESIGNER
ELLEN ZAHOREC

J ust looking at this pretty sit-upon makes you want to relive your scouting days, roasting marshmallows around a campfire and singing! Updated with bright vinyl, your sit-upon will come in very handy for picnics on the grass or chilly stone seats. This is an easy and fun project for kids to make, too.

INSTRUCTIONS

1. Glue your images onto the heavy paper right side up, unless you're working with an old poster. Let dry.

2. With the ruler and pencil, measure and mark lines lengthwise down the glued paper or the poster, spacing the lines ½ inch (1.3 cm) apart. Use the craft knife or scissors to carefully cut slits through the lines without going all the way to the edge of the paper.

3. Use the scissors to cut about 40 ½-inch-wide (102.87) strips from more of the decorative paper. Lay half the strips on the table, parallel with edges touching,

and tape down one end with the masking tape to hold in place. Use the other strips to weave over one, then under one, forming a checkerboard pattern.

4. When you've finished weaving, machine-stitch all four edges to keep it from unravelling. A wide zig-zag stitch looks particularly nice.

5. Cut a 20 x 23-inch (50.8 by 58.4 cm) piece of the vinyl, and trim the edges with the pinking shears for a decorative edge.

6. Center the woven paper piece on the vinyl, wrong sides together. Neatly fold the edges of the vinyl over the edge of the

woven paper, mitering the corners. Glue the vinyl in place and let dry.

7. Use the awl or ice pick to pierce holes along all four edges of the vinyl and paper assembly, spacing the holes ½ inch (1.3 cm) apart.

8. Lace the plastic lacing or string through the holes in a simple, continuous whip-stitch, up and over the edge. Lace three sides closed, leaving one of the short ends open.

9. Stuff about 10 layers of folded newspaper into the sit-upon, then lace the open end closed, making a neat knot on its underside.

MATERIALS

Plain canvas seat and back panels
for director's chair

Director's chair frame

TOOLS AND SUPPLIES

Thin, compressed sponges* (the kind that
expand in water)

Dowel, 1-inch (2.5 cm) diameter (optional)

Fine-tip permanent marker

Scissors

Pencil

Textile ink or paint, in roller-ball or jar form, in
yellow, green, blue, violet, red, and pink

Paintbrush (optional)

Plate

Piece of cardboard, 5 or 6 inches (12.7 or 15.2
cm) long

Paper towels

Clothes iron

*Sponge shapes are also available at craft
stores.

DIRECTOR'S CHAIRS IN BLOOM

DESIGNER
ELLEN ZAHOREC

A *canvas director's chair
is one of the simplest, most
mobile solutions for
garden seating. Do you
have one that's worn
around the edges, or just
too, too boring? You can
easily give it a "new" seat
and back by sponging on
paint in the shapes of
flowers. Use vibrant reds
and pinks for a lively
effect, or rich blues and
purples for quiet
and calm.*

INSTRUCTIONS

1. With the pen, draw flower shapes on the sponges. Refer to the photographs to create a lozenge shape for the leaves, and simple tulip, poppy, and daisy shapes. To make the iris, draw a shape on the sponge that looks like a section from an orange. Use one end of the dowel, or cut a round piece of sponge about as big as a quarter, to create the flower centers.

2. Cut out the shapes with the scissors.

3. Remove the seat and back from the chair, or remove them from their packaging, and lay them on a flat surface. Use the pencil to lightly sketch where you want to paint the flowers and leaves. To achieve the look shown in the photograph, create overlap in the rows of flowers.

4. Sponge or brush the ink or paint onto the plate. Lightly tap a sponge shape into the paint, and press it onto the canvas. Blot excess paint with the paper towels. Continue to print the flowers, overlapping them at the edges. Print the leaves next. Finish by printing the flower stems, using the edge of the piece of cardboard. Allow to dry.

5. Heat-set the printed design with the clothes iron.

Chapter XI

Shade and Accessories

Above: On a hot summer day, the most logical place for a garden seat is under a giant shade tree. If you don't have years to wait for that tree to grow, however, you have other options.

Shade is probably the single most important factor affecting the comfort of your garden seating. And in today's stressed world, we also retreat to our gardens to enjoy delicious peace and privacy.

You probably already know the spots in your yard that tend to get the most sun or stay the coolest throughout the year. In brief, northern and eastern exposures are cool, south is always warm, and west can be unbearable after a hot summer afternoon. If you want a west-facing seat so you can enjoy the sunset, plan to block at least some of the harsh midafternoon sun by installing a canopy or an umbrella. You may want to create a sheltered, sunny spot where you can sit and enjoy the fragrances of your flower garden; if so, planting or building a windbreak is easy!

Thick hedges and shrubs are ideal for creating sheltered alcoves in the garden; plant one main hedge, then other hedges perpendicular to it. If you're short on time, choose low-maintenance varieties that require only light pruning to keep their shape. Evergreens are a practical year-round solution because they don't lose their leaves. There are also some deciduous shrubs that will continue to give shelter in the winter because their branches grow so thickly. These include viburnum *(Viburnum)*, forsythia *(Oleaceae)*, and winter honeysuckle *(Lonicera fragrantissima)*.

Fragrant, sheltering vines and garden seating just seem to go together, don't they? Climbing hydrangea *(Hydrangea petiolaris)*, honeysuckle *(Lonicera)*, climbing roses *(Rosa)*, Carolina jessamine *(Gelsimium sempervirens)*, clematis *(Clematis)*, and jasmine *(Jasminum)* create wonderful shade and shelter when they grow on a supporting trellis or arbor. Check the vine's growth habits; wisteria *(Wisteria)*, and trumpet vine *(Campsis radicans)* are vigorous growers that need strong supports.

Building an arbor or pergola can be a daunting proposition with all those columns and cross beams. Why not copy the earliest arbors by interlacing the tops of trees or shrubs over your seating area? You can also construct the Morning Glory Garden Bench on page 154, using arched wire fencing to create the world's simplest built-in trellis. Plant it with quick-climbing, flowering annuals such as morning glories *(Ipomoea)*, moonflowers *(Ipomoea alba)*, or hyacinth bean *(Dolichos lablab)*, or float a piece of fabric over the top to create instant shade.

Ready-made objects can provide easy shade solutions. You can always bolt an umbrella to the back of a chair. If you have a shabby sun umbrella or a rain umbrella that has seen better days, why not remove the fabric and turn it into a mini-trellis, growing quick vines up the handle and along the "fingers" of the skeleton? Is there an old gate quietly rusting in your storage shed? Install it in the ground next to a seat that could use some shelter, and plant it with quick-growing vines for an almost instant wind screen.

The flowering shrub Rose of Sharon *(Hibiscus syriacus)* grows to 12 feet (3.6 m) tall, and is easily trained to form an arbor.

MATERIALS

For the trellis bench:

Roll of galvanized, vinyl-coated, 24-inch-wide (61 cm) wire fencing with 2 x 3-inch (5.1 x 7.6 cm) mesh openings

5 pieces 2 x 2 x 8 pressure-treated (PT) wood approved for ground contact, or hardwood

5 pieces 1 x 2 x 8 PT or hardwood

1 piece 2 x 4 x 8 PT or hardwood

2 pieces 1 x 6 x 8 PT or hardwood

For the bench cushion:

One piece of 54-inch-wide (137.16 cm) cotton polyester duck fabric, 53 inches (134.62 cm) long, in a forest green color

Foam cushion form, 24 x 48 x 2 inches (61 x 121.92 x 5.1 cm) thick

TOOLS AND SUPPLIES

For the trellis bench:

Protective gloves

Wire cutters

Ruler or tape measure

Fine-tip permanent marker

Power drill with ⅛- and ¼-inch (3 mm and 6 mm)

Phillips head bits

C-clamps, 5-inch (12.7 cm)

Triangle or carpenter's square

Hammer

A willing friend

Crescent wrench

Miter box (optional)

Handsaw (optional)

MORNING GLORY GARDEN BENCH WITH WIRE FENCE TRELLIS

DESIGNER
JANE WILSON

This is one of the easiest
bench-and-trellis combinations
we've ever seen!
Wire fencing is a snap to use to form
the arch, and you can plant it with
morning glories or other quick-growing
vines, or throw fabric over it
for instant shade. You can also
modify the design to make a longer
bench for a comfy spot to stretch out
and take a nap. Just increase
the length of the bench slats.
Directions are also given for making
an easy covered cushion for your bench.

TOOLS AND SUPPLIES

For the bench cushion:

Tape measure

Scissors

Straight pins

Thread to match fabric

Sewing machine

Electric iron

Can of spray-on water repellent for fabric

HARDWARE

44 #8 Phillips head wood screws, 1½ inches (3.8 cm) long

4 bolts, ¼-inch (6 mm) diameter and 4 inches (10.2 cm) long, with 4 matching nuts

4 8d nails, 3 inches (7.6 cm) long

12 6d nails, 2 inches (5.1 cm) long

CUT LIST

Code	Description	Qty	Materials and Dimensions
A	Arch uprights	4	2 x 2 PT or hardwood, 5' long
B	Upright supports	4	1 x 2 PT or hardwood, 5' long
C	Cross braces	2	2 x 4 PT or hardwood, 2' long
D	Bench slats	4	1 x 6 PT or hardwood, 4' long
E	Inner arch	6	2 x 2 PT or hardwood, 2 feet long crosspieces
F	Outer arch	6	1 x 2 PT or hardwood, 2' long crosspieces
G	Mitered bench support	4	2 x 2 PT or hardwood, 1' long supports with 45°miters

INSTRUCTIONS

Making the Trellis Bench

1. Wearing the protective gloves, use the wire cutters to cut a 16-foot length (4.8 m) of the wire fencing from the roll.

2. Refer to figure 1. Sandwich each cut end of the wire fencing between a pair of the 5-foot (1.5 m) 2 x 2 arch uprights (A) and a pair of the 5-foot 1 x 2 upright supports (B), with their sides flush on the outer edges. All the 1 x 2 supports (B) should be on top, on one side of the fencing, and the 2 x 2 uprights (A) on the bottom, with the fencing in between. Use the ruler and marker to indicate pilot holes 2 inches (5.1 cm) in from the ends of each support (B), and drill the pilot holes with the ⅛-inch (3 mm) bit, taking care to avoid the wire. Sink the wood screws through the pilot holes to secure each "sandwich."

3. While the assembly is still flat on the ground with the 1 x 2 upright supports (B) on top, you'll attach the inner and outer arch crosspieces (E and F). On the top side of the assembly, position a 1 x 2 outer arch crosspiece (F) flush against the inner ends of the two arch supports (B). Slip a 2 x 2 inner arch crosspiece (E) underneath, centering it under the 1 x 2 (F) with the wire fencing in between. Clamp together with the C-clamps, and secure with a wood screw at each end. Remove the clamps. Repeat on the other side of the assembly, against the other two arch supports.

4. Use the ruler to measure 7 inches (17.8 cm) in from the arch supports on each side. At each 7-inch (17.8 cm) point, repeat the "sandwich" assembly

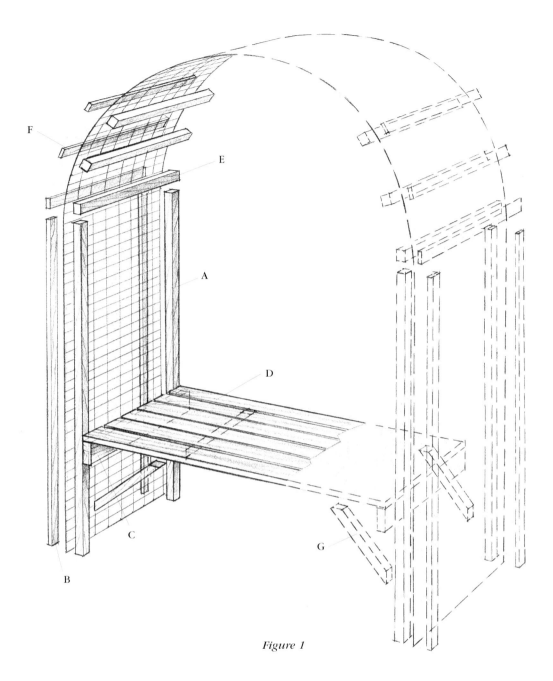

Figure 1

of 1 x 2 (B) fencing, and 2 x 2 (A). Measure in another 7 inches (17.8 cm) from each assembly, and install two more "sandwiches." You should now have six of these assemblies installed along the fencing. When you stand the arch up, the 2 x 2 uprights (A) will be on the inside of the standing arch, where you'll attach cross braces (C), which in turn will support the bench slats (D).

5. Flip the trellis assembly over so the 2 x 2 uprights (A) and 2 x 2 inner arch crosspieces (E) are on top. Use the ruler and marker to measure and mark 16 inches in from the end of each upright (A). Place a 2 x 4 cross brace (C) at the marks on a pair of the 2 x 2 uprights (A), positioning the cross braces on the outside of the marks. Use the triangle or square to make sure the cross brace is square to the uprights, so the bench

will be level when it's installed. Clamp together with the C-clamps.

6. Refer to figure 2. Now you'll install a 4-inch (10.2 cm) bolt at each end of both crosspieces (C) to strengthen the joins. About 1 inch (2.5 cm) below the edge of the crosspiece (C), drill a ¼-inch (6 mm) hole through all three pieces (A, B, and C). Slide in the bolt so that its nut end will be inside the arch,

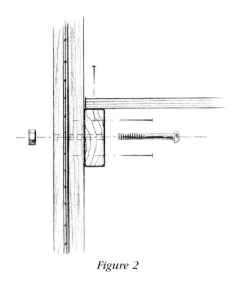

Figure 2

9. Lay the arch on its side, and fit a support (G) up in each corner below the bench. Nail in place with the 2-inch (5.1 cm) 6d nails, using two nails on each end of each support. Stand the bench up, making sure it's level. Plant morning glories for daytime color and moonflowers for evening scent, and enjoy!

Making the Bench Cushion

1. The finished bench cushion will be 2 inches (5.1 cm) thick and measure 24 x 48 inches (61 x 121.92 cm). Use the tape measure and scissors to measure and cut a piece of fabric measuring 51 inches (129.54 cm) across and 53 inches (134.62 cm) long. This includes extra material for ½-inch (1.3 cm) seam allowances and the thickness of the finished cushion.

2. Fold the fabric over, right side in. Use the straight pins to fasten the longest edge together.

3. Refer to fig. 4. Thread the sewing machine and sew a ½-inch (1.3 cm) seam (A) along the longest edge, leaving a 10-inch (25.4 cm) opening in the

and tighten the nut with the wrench. To further stabilize the connection, hammer in a 3-inch (7.6 cm) 8d nail about 1½ inches (3.8 cm) below the bolt, so the nail passes through the crossbrace (C) and into the upright (A). Remove the clamps. Repeat to install the other three bolts.

7. With the help of a friend, form an arch from the wire and wood assembly, with the inner arch crosspieces (E) inside the arch. Pull the bottom of the arch together until a bench slat (D) can rest on the crosspieces (C), spanning the inside of the arch at both

ends. The outside edges of the two outer bench slats (D) should be flush with the edges of the crosspieces (C). Screw the slats to the crosspieces, using two screws at each end. Place the two remaining slats (D) inside on the crosspieces, spacing all the slats approximately ³⁄₁₆ inch (4.8 mm) apart. Secure with screws.

8. Now you'll cut the mitered bench supports (G) from the remaining 2 x 2. As shown in figure 3, use the miter box and handsaw to cut a 45° angle on one end, then make four more opposing 45° cuts 12 inches (30.5 cm) apart to create four supports mitered at both ends.

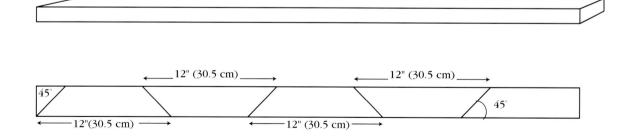

Figure 3

middle. Remove the pins, and lightly press the seam open with the iron. Now center the seam (A) in the "tube" of material, and sew ½-inch (1.3 cm) seams along the short edges (B) to close up both ends (see fig. 5). Press the seams open with the iron.

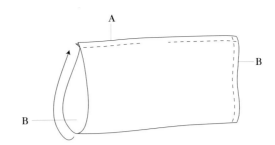

Figure 4

4. Now you'll create the four corners of the seat cushion using a simple mitering technique. With the cover still wrong side out and the longest seam centered, twist the fabric diagonally at one corner, so the raw edge of one of the short seams is centered in the corner, as shown in fig. 6. Pin together, and use the tape measure to measure in from the corner, along the centered seam, the same distance as the thickness of the cushion insert. Sew a seam at that point, inside the corner, from one side of the corner to the other. Remove the pins. Repeat with the other corner and the other short seam. Use the scissors to trim excess material from the corners.

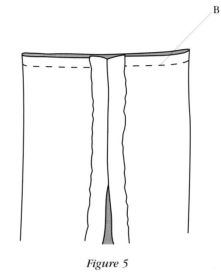

Figure 5

5. Turn the cover right side out. Make sure the raw edges of the opening in the long seam are tucked inside, and sew a ¼-inch (6 mm) seam on either side of the opening to hold the raw edges inside.

6. Slip the foam cushion form into the cover through the opening.

7. Spray the cushion with the water repellent according to package directions, and allow to dry. Install on the bench seat.

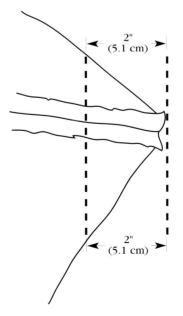

2"
(5.1 cm)

2"
(5.1 cm)

Figure 6

EASY SHADE LEAN-TO

What do you do if you already have a garden seat in the perfect location, but it's a bit too hot and sunny? You can use locally harvested reed, river cane, bamboo, and grasses to create one of the easiest and most natural shade solutions you'll ever find.

MATERIALS AND TOOLS

Cut reed, cane, and/or bamboo in 6- to 8-foot (1.8 x 2.4 m) lengths, in a quantity sufficient to create two "walls" of the lean-to

Pruners or handsaw

Twine

Shovel

Rocks

A helpful friend

Freshly cut bamboo, or living bamboo plants

Cut ornamental grasses

INSTRUCTIONS

1. First, you'll make the parts for a light, trellislike structure to help the lean-to maintain its shape. Select pieces of the reed, 1 or ½ inch (2.5 or 1.3 cm) in diameter. Use the pruners or saw to trim a crosspiece from the reed, making it about as long as the garden seat you wish to cover. Trim two more pieces to a length equal to the front-to-back depth of the seat. These will serve as side supports for the walls. Set aside.

2. Divide the remaining reed into three piles. You'll use two of the piles to create the lean-to walls. The third pile should be smaller. Gather the materials of the third pile together at one end, with the ends flush, and use a piece of the twine to securely lash everything together.

3. Use the shovel to dig a shallow depression in the earth behind the bench, and stand the lashed-together cane up in it, bracing it with the rocks to stabilize it. Fan out the canes. Place the crosspiece you cut in step 1 against the cane, about 4 feet (1.2 m) above the ground and parallel to the ground, and use the twine to tie the canes to the crosspiece, spacing out the canes.

4. Spread out the reed from one of the two large piles flat on the ground, with the bottom ends spread out but flush with each other. Place one of the side supports on top, about 4 feet (1.2 m) from the bottom end. Adjust the reed so it spans the length of the support, and use the twine in a rough in-and-out weave to connect the reed to the support. Repeat with the second pile of reed and second support.

5. With your friend's help, raise the two reed-and-support wall structures, placing one on each end of the bench, and gently lean them together so they touch at the top. Tie the back ends of the side supports to each end of the crosspiece.

6. Gently intertwine the reeds at the top, and use more twine to secure them if desired.

7. Decorate the sides and top of your lean-to with the freshly cut bamboo and ornamental grasses. Alternatively, you can actually plant living bamboo along the back and sides of the lean-to for continuous "green" decoration.

MATERIALS

½ yard (.45 m) textured, sheer fabric for draperies, 45-inch (114.3 cm) width, in red, pink, or white for the flower stamens

Petal template on page 165

Thread in colors to match the stamens, petals, and bract

1 piece of crib quilt batting, 45 x 60 inches (114.3 x 152.4 cm)

1 yard lining fabric, 45-inch (114.3 cm) width

1 yard polyester fabric, 45-inch (114.3 cm) width, in red, pink, or maroon for the flower petals

¼ yard (.23 m) fabric, in dark green for the flower bract

TOOLS AND SUPPLIES

Tape measure or ruler

Pencil, chalk, or fabric marker

Scissors

Straight pins

Sewing machine

Crochet hook or chopstick (optional)

Photocopier

Fine-tip permanent marker

Dressmaker's carbon paper (optional)

Tracing wheel (optional)

Upholstery needle

DOROTHY LAMOUR, WHERE ARE YOU? GIANT HIBISCUS PILLOWS

DESIGNER
Jane Wilson

*T*he very essence of
tropical glamour, these
pillows are big enough
to seat a grown-up and
they make great throws
for outdoor parties.
Scatter a few around,
put on some music
with a Latin beat, and
let the fun begin!

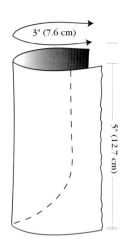

3" (7.6 cm)

5" (12.7 cm)

Figure 1

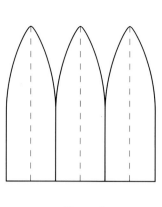

Figure 2

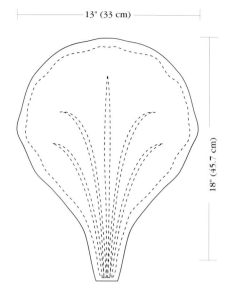

13" (33 cm)

18" (45.7 cm)

Figure 4

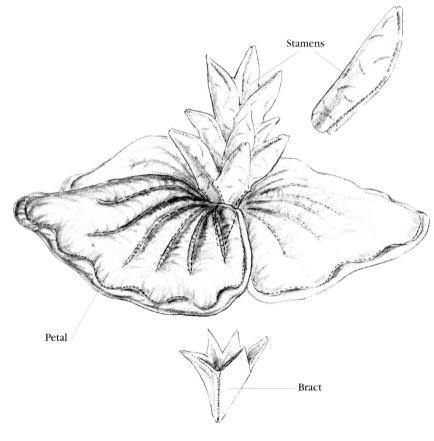

Stamens

Petal

Bract

Figure 3

INSTRUCTIONS

1. First, you'll make the "stamens" that form the center section of the pillow. Use the tape measure and pencil to measure and mark the drapery sheer in the following pieces: five 3 x 5-inch (7.6 cm x 12.7 cm) pieces, three 3 x 9-inch (7.6 x 22.9 cm) pieces, and three 3 x 12-inch (7.6 x 30.5 cm) pieces. Cut them out with the scissors.

2. Fold the 3-inch (7.6 cm) side of each cutout piece in half as shown in fig. 1, right side in, and pin together with the straight pins. Use the pencil to lightly trace a shape on the fabric like the one in the illustration.

3. Thread the sewing machine, and use it to sew a ¼-inch (6 mm) seam along the outline you traced on the fabric, leaving the end open. Use the scissors to trim the seam, cutting a diagonal on the corner and small notches along the curve. Be careful not to cut into the seam.

4. Refer to fig. 2. Turn the sewn pieces right side out. Lay the 5-inch-long (12.7 cm) pieces flat on the work surface, centering the seam on top as shown. Use the machine to sew together the pieces, seaming together only about half of their straight side edges and leaving the top, curved sections free. Repeat steps 2 through 4 to make 9-inch (22.9 cm) and 12-inch-long (30.5 cm) groups of stamens varying the length of the material accordingly.

5. Nest the three groups of stamens with the longest in the middle, surrounded by the mid-length stamens, and the shortest on the outside (see fig. 3). Set aside.

6. Now you'll make the hibiscus petals. Use the photocopier to enlarge the petal template in figure 4 to the dimensions indicated. Make note of where you'll leave an opening on the seam.

7. Stack two layers of batting, a layer of lining, two layers of the polyester fabric turned right side in, and a layer of lining.

8. Lay the petal template on top and use the marker to trace around it, being sure to mark the seam opening. Remove the template. Pin the layers together with the straight pins, and use the scissors to cut them out, leaving extra material around the edges so you can add a ½-inch (1.3 cm) seam allowance around the traced outline. Make a total of five cut-out petal "stacks."

9. Thread the sewing machine, set it to eight stitches per inch (2.5 cm), and sew a seam directly on the traced outline of each petal. Don't sew the open-

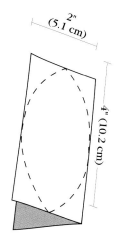

Figure 5

ing closed. Use the scissors to trim the seam allowance to ¼ inch (6 mm), cutting the corners on the diagonal and cutting tiny notches in the curved seam allowance. Be careful not to cut into the seam.

10. Use your hands to open up the petal slightly at the opening, between the two layers of polyester fabric. Sew the polyester fabric on the bottom layer to the batting on the bottom, sewing along the edge of the opening. Do not sew the opening closed.

11. Turn the petal right side out through the opening you left in the seam. Use the crochet hook to poke out the corners if necessary. The petal will have a side that doesn't show the inner seams prominently; this will be the "face" of the petal. Position the template over the petal, and use the carbon paper and tracing wheel, if desired, to mark the quilting lines in the center and perimeter of the petal.

12. With the machine set to eight stitches per inch (2.5 cm), machine-stitch a ¼-inch (6 mm) seam around the petal as marked on the template. Turn the raw edges of the opening you

left in the seam allowance to the inside, being sure to run the quilting seam close enough to close the opening. Sew along the quilting lines too.

13. Place the edges of two petals face together, and sew their two edges together by hand at their inner ends and midpoint. Use shallow stitches that join the fabric but not the batting. Continue to join the sides of the petals until they form a cup.

14. To make the "bract" that holds the lower ends of the petals underneath the flower, fold the forest green fabric right side together, and cut out five shapes as shown in fig. 5. With the green thread in the machine, sew a ¼-inch (6 mm) seam along the curved edges, leaving an opening to turn them right side out. Use the scissors to trim the seam and corners, and turn each piece right side out. Use the green thread in the machine to sew the openings closed and to sew the lower edges of the bract components together, forming a cup shape.

15. Fit the stamens into the center of the sewn-together petal cup, and slide the bract over the bottom. Use the upholstery needle and green thread to sew all the pieces together at the bottom. The finished pillow will measure about 30 inches (76.2 cm) across, with a circumference of about 90 inches (228.6 cm).

MATERIALS

4 rhododendron branch uprights, each 7½ to 8 feet (2.25 to 2.4 m) tall and 2½ inches (6.4 cm) in diameter

4 branches to serve as rafters, each 3 feet (.9 m) long

14 to 18 crosspieces, each 2 feet (.6 m) long

Assorted smaller branches for filler

4 pieces of rebar, each 2 feet (.6 m) long

Shrub or vine of your choice (*eleagnus* is shown in the photo)

TOOLS AND SUPPLIES

Pruning saw

Measuring tape

Fine-tip permanent marker

Assorted cement coated nails, 2 to 3 inches (5.1 to 7.6 cm) long

Hammer

Wire

Shovel

Plant ties

Pruners

INSTRUCTIONS

1. Use the pruning saw to cut the branches to the lengths specified. To create the arched shape of the arbor, the uprights themselves should gently arch. When the uprights are joined, they'll create a walk-through 3 to 4 feet (.9 to 1.2 m) wide.

SIMPLE RUSTIC ARBOR

DESIGNER
J. DABNEY PEEPLES

The rhododendron branches used to construct this arbor create an inviting arched shape, though you can use many different woods for varying effects. **Elaeagnus** *usually grows as a large, sprawling shrub. The shrub's runners were easily pruned and trained to grow up and over the arbor structure, covering it beautifully with silvery gray leaves within a couple of years. As a bonus, it has delicious berries and gives off a wonderful fragrance.*

2. To make the sides of the arbor, lay out two of the uprights on the work surface, making sure the arched bends are oriented toward the same direction. Use the measuring tape and marker to mark 16-inch-wide (40.6 cm) intervals on the uprights. Using nails of a length that will penetrate both pieces without going all the way through, nail the 2-foot (.6 m) crosspieces to the two uprights, making a ladderlike form. If the nail does pierce both branches, bend it over with the hammer, and rust will eventually help disguise it. Complete the other side of the arbor with the remaining two uprights and crosspieces.

3. Place the two finished upright sections on their sides, so the tops touch and the sides are parallel. Nail the rafters about 1 foot (30.5 cm) below the top of the uprights, then nail two crosspieces to each rafter to connect them even more securely to the upright.

4. Stand the arbor on its feet, and nail the smaller, filler branches to the sides and top. If you place the smaller branches creatively, you can make it look as though the arbor grew where it stands.

5. Place the arbor in your garden. To secure it, drive the rebar into the ground at the points where the uprights touch the ground, leaving about 1 foot (30.5 cm) of the rebar above ground. Use the wire to attach the uprights to the rebar.

6. Dig a hole three times as wide as the root ball of the shrub or vine, at the base of the arbor on the outside. Plant the shrub or vine, and water and feed it as recommended. As it grows, attach it to the arbor with the plant ties, and prune new growth to encourage it to grow up and over the arbor.

Extra- Comfy Loveseat Templates

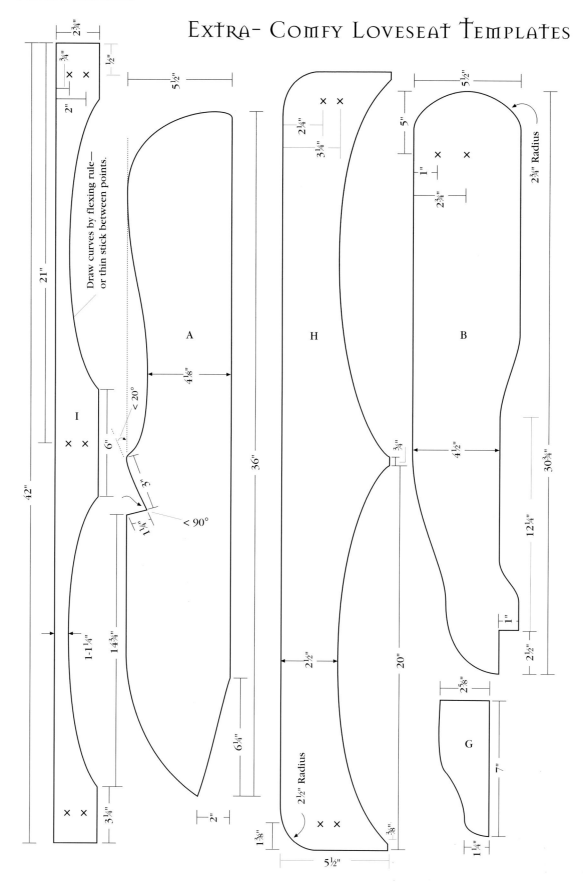

2¾"

¾"

½"

2"

5½"

21"

Draw curves by flexing rule—
or thin stick between points.

A

< 20°

4⅛"

6"

I

3"

< 90°

1¼"

36"

42"

14¾"

1-1¼"

3¼"

2"

6¼"

2¼"

3¼"

H

5½"

5"

1"

2¾"

B

2¾" Radius

¾"

4½"

30¾"

12¼"

1"

2½"

2⅝"

G

7"

1¼"

20"

2½"

2½" Radius

1⅜"

⅜"

5½"

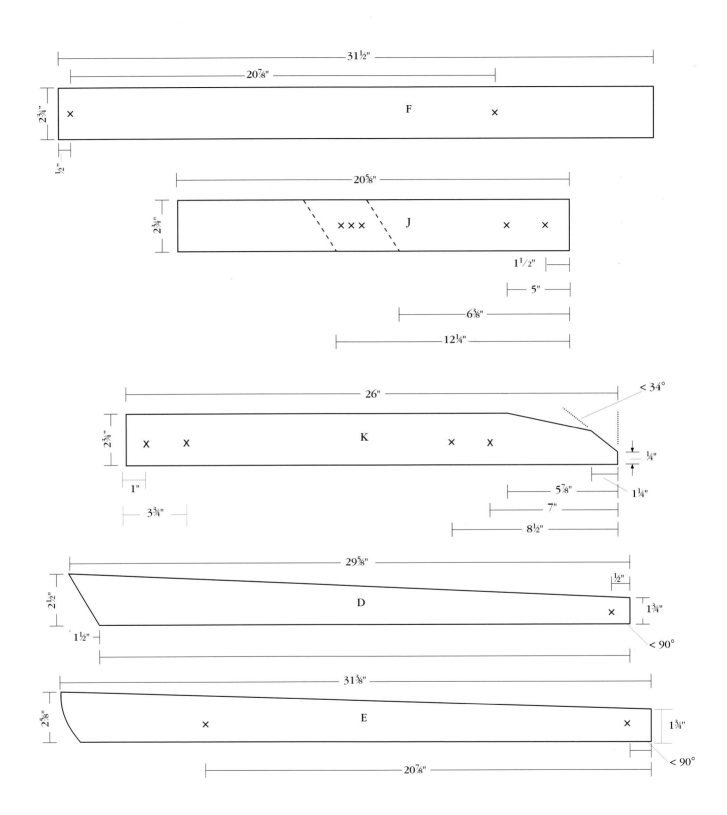

Note: *For metric equivalents, refer to chart on page 172*
Templates are not to scale

DESIGNERS AND CONTRIBUTORS

ROBERT CHEATHAM
began his artistic career designing and building sculptural furniture from wood. He later adopted concrete and ferrocement techniques, which he uses in his studio and garden constructions, often adding mosaic tile and painted finishes. <zeug@pd.ord>

NORMA CHEREN
brought elements from the fiber arts, food arts, glassblowing, woodworking, and blacksmithing to the creation of her garden. Her understanding of color, texture, shape, scale, and joie de vivre all combine in her life philosophy, "Art is what an artist makes." She lives in Atlanta, Georgia, and is building a house in Celo, North Carolina.

DEREK FELL
is a widely published garden photographer with more awards from the Garden Writers' Association of America than any other person. His own garden, Cedaridge Farm in Pennsylvania, has also won numerous awards for landscape design.

GEORGE HARRISON
has been a professional woodworker for 37 years. He lives in the historic Ox Creek area of Weaverville, North Carolina.

DOUG HAYS & PENNY CASH
work from their joint Florida studio to produce works of art in steel, glass, and clay. Partners in life and art, they move freely among their mediums and will soon introduce new pieces incorporating blown, fused, and cast glass with raku and steel. <hayscash@mail.hayscash.com> 26119 Troon Ave, Mt. Plymouth, FL, 32776

ALAN MICHAEL HESTER
has been a custom woodworker since 1978 and works mostly in hardwoods. He lives in Asheville with his wife and son. Hester's Lothlorien, 244B Swannanoa River Road, Asheville NC 28805, (828) 258-1445.

EDITH HOWARD
has been a contributing designer to previous Lark Books, including *The Well-Decorated Garden, (1999)* courtesy of Applewood Crafts, Asheville, North Carolina.

SHERRI WARNER HUNTER
is a sculptor who has been working with concrete for a decade. Her large-scale concrete and mosaic public sculptures are featured at the Memphis/Shelby County Public Library, Nashville International Airport, and Vanderbilt Children's Hospital in Tennessee. She is the author of the Lark book, *Creating With Concrete: Yard Art, Sculpture, and Garden Projects.* She lives in Bell Buckle, Tennessee with her husband, Martin.

JOHNNY LEE JONES
is a self-taught furniture refinisher/builder whose store, Classic Antiques, in Raleigh, North Carolina, has been in business for 21 years. He specializes in architectural iron.

LISA MANDLE
is the owner and principal designer of Only One, a custom clothing and accessories business in Madison County, North Carolina. Before she moved to North Carolina, she was selected as one of the top 10 designers in Washington, D.C.

RAY MARTIN
is co-author of *Building Garden Furniture*, published by Lark Books and Sterling Publishing Co., Inc., in 1993.

CHRISTOPHER D. MELLO
is a horticulturist by trade (but prefers to call himself a gardener), and he gained much of his experience on the grounds of the historic Biltmore Estate in his hometown of Asheville, North Carolina. He is also an accomplished metal sculptor and floral designer. His studio is open to the public on Saturdays and by appointment. 9 Riverside Drive, Asheville, NC, 28801, (828) 255-8648

JEAN TOMASO MOORE
has been creating art in various forms for as long as she can remember. A part-time multi-media artist, she lives in Asheville with her patient and humble husband. <LeaningTowerArt@aol.com>

ENID MUNROE
is the author of *An Artist in the Garden: A Guide to Creative and Natural Gardening.* (Henry Holt and Company, 1994). Her paintings, drawings, and collages are in numerous private and corporate collections. She lives in Fairfield, Connecticut, with her husband and co-gardener, Harry.

ERIC O'LEARY
is an accomplished ceramicist and member of the New Hampshire Potters' Guild, League of New Hampshire Craftsmen, and National Council on Education for Ceramic Arts. His work is in the collections of the Museum of Fine Arts, Boston, the White House, and the Currier Museum. Tariki Studio, P.O. Box 172, 12 Bean Road, Meriden, NH 03770, (603) 469-3243

J. DABNEY PEEPLES
is president and senior landscape/garden designer of J. Dabney Peeples Design Associates, Inc., of Easley, South Carolina. The firm works throughout the Southeast. Peeples' residence, a 30-acre farm in Easley, serves as a design studio.

DANIEL O. PETERSEN

has 23 years of experience in the tree care industry. His company, Petersen Tree and Landscape Management, is located in Swannanoa, North Carolina.

ROB PULLEYN

is President of Lark Books, and is usually a very hands-off manager. But when the spirit moves him, he can't help using his hands to create projects for our books. He lives in the mountains of western North Carolina.

LEE RANKIN

is co-author of *Building Garden Furniture*, published by Lark Books and Sterling Publishing Co., Inc., in 1993.

RANDALL RAY

works from his furniture studio in Asheville, North Carolina. He pursues woodworking in many different forms, including boatbuilding, cabinetry, restoration, reproduction, and contemporary works. <jrcshop@aol.com>

RICHARD CHARLES REAMES

owns and operates Arborsmith Studios in Williams, Oregon, where he designs, plants, bends, and grafts trees to form living houses, furniture, fences, gazebos, and other constructions. Author of the book *How to Grow a Chair: The Art of Tree Trunk Topiary* (Arborsmith Studios, 1995), he has been practicing "arborsculpture" for more than seven years. <arborstu@magick.net>

JANICE SHIELDS

has worked as a dress shop manager and foreign car mechanic, and she credits her mother with her love of tinkering. She started her rustic furnishings business in 1995, and works with saplings and oriental bittersweet vines. Cut It Out, 326 Old Stockbridge Road, Lenox, MA 01240, (413) 637-0400. <janice@heycutitout.com>

LAURA SPECTOR

has been building rustic furniture for six years. Her whimsical and romantic creations are inspired by the natural curves, twists, and knurls of oriental bittersweet vine. She markets her home and garden furniture through Laura Spector Rustic Design, Fairfield, Connecticut. <lsrustic@aol.com>

CAROL STANGLER

is an environmental artist. She lives in and maintains a studio in Asheville, North Carolina. Her work is featured in *Making the New Baskets,* published by Lark Books and Sterling Publishing Company, Inc. (1999). Carol is also the author of a book on crafting with bamboo to be published by Lark and Sterling in 2001.

TERI STEWART

has broad experience as a sculptor, producer, and curator including exhibits at Atlanta Century Gallery, Ra Rising Gallery, Henrietta Eggleston Hospital for Children, and DeepSouthCon 26. She collaborates with numerous artists including her studio partner Serey Andree. Teri also runs the environmental studies program at Horizons School in Dekalb County, Georgia.

JIMMY STRAELA

makes artwork from found materials and old lumber salvaged from house demolitions or burn piles. He also uses granite from a quarry in nearby Tinytown, Georgia. Architectural Resurrections, 425½ Hill Street, Athens, GA 30601, (706) 338-7257. <laurastraehla@yahoo.com>

TERRY TAYLOR

specializes in creating art for the garden using the pique-assiette, or shard art, technique. Terry is known for his willingness to try any craft, and does a fabulous job at whatever he tries. He collects, creates, and carves from his home in Asheville, North Carolina.

SUE AND ADAM TURTLE

publish the international journal *Temperate Bamboo Quarterly*. They also offer courses in working with bamboo at Earth Advocates Research Farm and operate "Our" Bamboo Nursery, a wholesale source of landscape-grade bamboo plants in Summertown, Tennessee, (931) 964-4151.

JANE WILSON

spent many years as a studio designer, after studying art history and design at East Tennessee University and technical drawing and drafting at Eastern Kentucky University. 76 Riverview Drive, Asheville, NC, 28806 (828)281-0465. Email <janewilson34@hotmail.com> or visit her website <www.janewilson-studio.com>

CYNTHIA WYNN

began metalworking in 1990. Her work started winning awards during her second semester at the University of North Carolina at Asheville, and two years later Wynn had her own shop. She did the installation of the Rework Museum in Key West, Florida, and she continues to divide her time among Key West, Asheville, and street festivals. 5517 5th Avenue, Key West, FL 33040, (305) 587-3753, or 6½ Riverside Dr., Asheville, NC 28801.

ELLEN ZAHOREC

is an internationally-exhibited, mixed-media artist and adjunct professor at Xavier University. She and her husband Alex Hughes own and operate Zahorec/Hughes Gallery in Cincinnati, Ohio. <ezahorec@aol.com>

Metric Conversion Table

Inches	Centimeters		Inches	Centimeters
⅛	3 mm		12	30
¼	6 mm		13	32.5
⅜	9 mm		14	35
1/2	1.3		15	37.5
⅝	1.6		16	40
¾	1.9		17	42.5
7/8	2.2		18	45
1	2.5		19	47.5
1¼	3.1		20	50
1½	3.8		21	52.5
1¾	4.4		22	55
2	5		23	57.5
2½	6.25		24	60
3	7.5		25	62.5
3½	8.8		26	65
4	10		27	67.5
4½	11.3		28	70
5	12.5		29	72.5
5½	13.8		30	75
6	15		31	77.5
7	17.5		32	80
8	20		33	82.5
9	22.5		34	85
10	25		35	87.5
11	27.5		36	90

Acknowledgments

People who love gardens and all things gardening-related are a special group of people, and I couldn't have written this book without them. Many thanks to the designers who created our how-to projects, to the friends who literally opened their homes and gardens to us, and to the artists and landscape architects who shared images of their work. I owe a special thank you to Dabney Peeples, Graham A. Kimak, and Arthur Campbell for their expertise and Southern hospitality.

I was fortunate to have technical, editorial, and artistic help from Jerald Snow, Joe Archibald, Kevin Barnes, and Perri Crutcher. Thank you as well to Evan Bracken for his photography, to artist Olivier Rollin for ces dessins magnifiques, and to Orrin Lundberg and Lark production assistant Hannes Charen for their informative visuals.

I'm also fortunate to work with colleagues here at Lark who share a common interest in making beautiful and meaningful books. Thank you, Terry Taylor, for reaching into that amazing Rolodex of yours, and thank you, Dana Irwin, for bringing a passion for excellence and a remarkable artistic eye to its art direction. The skills of assistant editors Veronika Alice Gunter, Heather Smith, Roper Cleland, and Emma Jones were essential. And finally, a big thank you to Lark's new woodworking guru Andy Rae, for his timely and expert advice. Glad you're here, Andy.

LOCATIONS:

Roger Bakeman, Atlanta, GA

Brad Lawley, Decatur, GA

Carolyn Krueger, Decatur, GA

Charles and Gail Jones, Greenville, SC

David and Geri Laufer, Roswell, GA

Don and Ellen Wall, Greer, SC

Mr. and Mrs. David Lichtenfelt, Easley, SC

Elizabeth Lide and Paul Kayhart, Atlanta, GA

Frank and Emme Gannon, Greer, SC

Heather Spencer and Charles Murray, Asheville, NC

Hedy Fischer and Randy Schull, Asheville, NC

James Hiram Malone, Atlanta, GA

Jasmine and Dr. Peter Gentling, Asheville, NC

John Cram, Asheville, NC

John and Mary Dinkel, Greer, SC

Norma Cheren, Decatur, GA

Patrick Bralick and Dr. Julie Newberg, Liberty, SC

Scott and Amy Eller, Salisbury, NC

Teri Stewart and Iris Hale, Atlanta, GA

Robin Van Valkenburgh, wa wië, Asheville, NC

Christopher Mello, Asheville, NC

LANDSCAPE ARCHITECTS & DESIGNERS:

J. Dabney Peeples and Graham A. Kimak, J. Dabney Peeples Design Associates, Inc., Easley, SC

Arborsmith Studios, Williams, OR

Jerald A. Snow, ASLA, Asheville, NC

Ken Smith, Landscape Architect, New York, NY

Landplan Studio, Fair Lawn, NJ

Martina Meyer Interior Design and Hawthorne Studio, Santa Fe, NM

Signe Nielsen Landscape Architect, New York, NY

Steven J. Young, ASLA, SJY Design, Oakland, CA

Terry Broussard, ASLA, Broussard Associates Landscape Architects, Clovis, CA

Photo Credits

Page 6: Ohme Gardens County Park, Wenatchee, WA; Charles Adams, photographer

Page 7: Ken Smith Landscape Architect, New York, NY; Betsy Pinover Schiff, photographer

Page 8 (bottom left), 39, 48 (right), 65 (top and middle): used with permission from Biltmore Estate, Asheville, North Carolina. Evan Bracken, photographer

Page 9 (bottom left): Signe Nielsen Landscape Architect, P.C., New York, NY; Signe Nielsen, photographer

Page 11 (top): Martina Meyer Interior Design, Santa Fe, NM; Hawthorne Studio—Don Gregg, photographer

Page 14 (top right), 15 (bottom right): J. Dabney Peeples Design Associates, Inc., Easley, SC; Graham A. Kimak, photographer

p. 14 (top left): Thom Gaines, photographer

p.15 (bottom right): J. Dabney Peeples Design Associates, Inc., Easley, SC.

p. 17 (top), 47, 84 (top and left), 85 (top right), 86 (top left), 87 (left), 151 (right): Richard Hasselberg, photographer

p. 17 (bottom left): Broussard Associates Landscape Architects, Clovis, CA; Terry Broussard, ASLA, architect; Larry Falke, photographer

p. 19 (top right), 151 (top left): Dana Irwin, photographer

p. 20 (top): Charles Mann Photography, Inc., Santa Fe, NM

p. 21, 22, 23, 24, 25, 45: Enid Munroe, photographer

p. 31, 32, 64 (top), 69: Janice Eaton Kilby, photographer

p. 43, 51: Derek Fell, photographer

p. 52, 53: Richard Charles Reames, photographer

p. 75 (top), 81: Robert Cheatham, photographer

p. 89: VNU Syndication, Hoofddorp, The Netherlands; George v.d. Wijngaard, photographer

p. 103, 107: VNU Syndication, Hoofddorp, The Netherlands; John van Groenendaal, photographer

p. 127 (bottom middle), 131: Hays Cash, Tampa, FL; Reed Photography, Umatilla, FL, photographer

p. 135: Chuck Pearson, Key West, FL, photographer

p. 141: VNU Syndication, Hoofddorp, The Netherlands; Peter Kooijman, photographer

p. 152 (left): Laura Spector, Laura Spector Rustic Designs, bench with market umbrella. Enid Munroe, photographer

p. 161: VNU Syndication, Hoofddorp, The Netherlands; Hanneke Reijbroek, photographer

Index